THE COST-CONSCIOUS COOK

by

Maggie Brogan

PAPERFRONTS

Typeset in 10pt Times Roman by One & A Half Graphics, Redhill, Surrey.
Printed in England by Clays Ltd, St Ives plc.

The *Paperfronts* series and the *Right Way* series are both published by Elliot Right Way Books, Brighton Road, Lower Kingswood, Tadworth, Surrey, KT20 6TD, U.K.

THE
COST-CONSCIOUS
COOK

Other cookery books in the Paperfront series

The After Work Cook*

The Stir Fry Cook

The Barbecue Cook

Uniform with this book

*By the same author

CONTENTS

INTRODUCTION

Sadly everything is so commercialised today that we expect to pay for most of our pleasures. Food is no exception. It was only when, like millions of others, I was forced to look at ways of cutting overheads that I realised what an enormous amount of money was disappearing into the coffers of major supermarkets.

Shopping is habit-forming and habits are hard to break. I was as guilty as anyone of buying ready-made cakes, pastry, sauces, salads, instant this, instant that and vast quantities of exotically packaged delicacies, commonly referred to as convenience foods. Of course they make cooking quicker and easier — but expensive.

Spending less is really a question of returning to basics. Years ago people had to make do. There were no State handouts and many women, faced with feeding a family on little money, became adept at making something out of nothing.

Bombarded as we are today by convenience food giants, many youngsters have never been taught, and even some adults have forgotten, that good food and a healthy diet are achieved by the creative use of a few basic raw materials.

Perhaps it takes a financial crisis to bring us to our senses. The desire to do without is no doubt a good thing. Hardship can mean the beginning of self-discovery, developing skills of which you never knew you were capable.

My objective has been to produce a main course to serve four people for little more than the cost of 20 cigarettes or, put another way, for the price of this book or a gallon of petrol.

Research has led me to people who were brought up in the depression of the 1930s and to those who lived through the Second World War when the choice of food was limited. Ideas have also been recalled from my own time at school and college, before the days when anyone who made bread was regarded with the same suspicion as someone from outer space!

Here then is a collection of recipes and cost-cutting ideas to help reduce your weekly housekeeping bill. However there is an added bonus; in many cases a cheaper diet makes for a healthier way of life.

The Western diet is implicated as a major cause of heart disease, some cancers, diabetes and gall stones — all problems which hardly exist in poorer countries.

Hardly a week goes by without some expert telling us what we should and shouldn't eat. Confused? Don't worry, so is everyone else. The eating game holds more contradictions than a Cabinet meeting!

There is certainly growing concern as to the effect that flavourings, colourings and preservatives have on health. On randomly picking a few convenience foods off the shelf, many contained an alarming list of 'E' numbers. Do you know what they all mean? I certainly don't! Is the modern convenient diet not only expensive but little more than a chemical cocktail?

I live by the traditional maxim that anything in moderation cannot be too harmful. If you eat a balance of fresh fruit and vegetables, dairy produce, lentils and beans, starchy foods like pasta, rice and home-baked bread and a little meat and fish you can't go far wrong. Wholesome home cooking certainly means less intake of highly processed or refined foods and artificial additives.

A meatless meal two or three times a week offers enormous opportunity to keep costs down. Fruit, vegetables, nuts, beans and lentils are much cheaper than meat or fish. And for the sceptics, vegetarian cookery has become very sophisticated indeed. Gone are the days when vegetarianism meant sawdust-dry nut roasts and tasteless lentil cutlets. In many recipes it is impossible to tell that you are not eating meat.

Living as we do today in a frantic age of hard-edged technology, when 'quicker' and 'disposable' are often taken to mean 'better' and 'convenient', more than ever we need to return to the basic sanity of simple and fundamental pleasures. In recent years there has been a trend back towards good old fashioned values so perhaps this is as good a time as any to recapture traditional culinary skills. Ignore the pressures of junk food advertising, and you will do wonders for your health and bank balance. Who knows, you could discover a whole new way of life!

1. COST-CUTTERS

Shop around: you will be amazed at the bargains to be had if you keep your eyes open! Although supermarkets are fairly competitive for basics like flour, margarine, milk and sugar, in my experience national chains are expensive for fresh produce, particularly meat, fruit and vegetables.

A short way from where I live in Bristol there is an excellent discount butcher and greengrocer, and similar shops have sprung up all over the country in recent years. Markets are another source of value-for-money produce.

With modern preserving and food production methods, and vast quantities of imported goods, just about anything is available all the year round. Although fruit and vegetables tend to be at their cheapest when in season (see Chapter 6 Vegetarian Meals), it pays to keep your eyes on shop displays because prices vary from day to day and shop to shop, with certain items being offered at prices you can't afford to miss.

A random example of some bargain buys which I regularly take advantage of includes bags of mixed peppers costing the same price usually charged for one; similar bags of aubergines; two cauliflowers for the price of one; and pound bags of mushrooms and tomatoes at half the cost you would expect to pay in a supermarket.

Good Butchers' Buys

Butchers' home-made sausages and sausagemeat knock spots off the commercially prepared kind and I've used these in all the sausage recipes (see Chapter 8 Meat). Bags of bacon bits are cheap, and ideal for recipes which demand chopped bacon. Any excess can be frozen in small lots for future use.

I usually find that most cuts of meat cost less from a butcher but it's worth checking prices yourself before buying. For example, look for supermarket meat marked 'reduced price' and 'special offer' and look in freezer cabinets for value-for-money pork steaks, New Zealand lamb and other meaty bits and pieces.

Tips To Stay Within Budget

Most people decide what to eat and then do the shopping. Yet by planning in reverse you will have more chance of keeping within budget. If, for example, you spot a bargain at the butcher or greengrocer, snap it up and then find a recipe to fit. Likewise look in your fridge/freezer/store cupboard each week to see what needs eating up and then find a recipe which uses those particular ingredients.

No Excuse For Wastage

If any oddments are in danger of ending up in the bin, use them first! The last few porridge oats of the winter could go into a Meat Loaf (see page 108); add the remains of a bag of sultanas to scones, a rice salad or a curry; chop a couple of bacon rashers into an omelette; peel the skin off a shrivelled apple and slice the flesh into a salad; use up odd vegetables in soups and stews and if, like mine, the remnants of your soft brown sugar have formed a solid block, melt it down for Flapjacks (see page 129).

Store Cupboard Flavourings

Although I aim in this book to keep occasional, and often

expensive, flavourings to a minimum I do recommend keeping a few multi-purpose items which are useful for adding flavour and interest to cheap meals. These include mayonnaise, tomato purée, yeast extract, stock cubes, a few spices, Worcestershire sauce and a tub of grated Parmesan cheese.

After the initial outlay, your weekly budget should gradually balance out because it is unlikely that everything will run out at once. I find it's cheaper to buy loose spices from a specialist shop and then fill my own jars, rather than buying pre-packed jars from supermarkets.

Money-Off Coupons

I used to consider these an enormous nuisance until I added up just how much money I was chucking in the bin! I now study my junk mail a bit more carefully. The average household receives a startling amount of money in special offers during the year so, if you use the products, use the coupons!

Christmas Clubs

Many butchers now run a savings plan to spread the cost of meat at Christmas. Fifty pence or so paid in a week could be worth thinking about.

Cash In On The Fruit Glut

On a warm summer weekend take the family on a pick-your-own-fruit trip. Children will love it, especially sneaking the odd strawberry out of the collection basket when they think no one is looking!

June and July are the best months to catch cheap home-grown strawberries, raspberries, redcurrants, blackcurrants, gooseberries and many varieties of vegetable. In autumn come blackberries (free!), tomatoes, plums and cooking apples.

An hour or so spent picking will certainly save money; prices are about half the shop rate. Alternatively, a drive into the country or even into the leafier suburbs will lead to any number of people selling, or almost giving away, fruit and vegetables at their gates.

Frozen Assets

Freezing your crop (if you possess a freezer) will set you up for the months ahead when fresh produce is expensive and scarce. (Or have a go at making jam and chutney — see Chapter 13, Gifts Good Enough To Eat.)

Raspberries, blackberries, gooseberries, blackcurrants, redcurrants and sliced cooking apples (peeled and cored first) all freeze well. For best results, freeze separately on baking trays and, when hard, pack into individual polythene bags.

Strawberries tend to go mushy if frozen and are best frozen as a purée and used to make ice cream, sorbet and sauces. Tomatoes too are best frozen as a sauce (see page 55 for Fresh Tomato Sauce).

Grow Your Own Herbs

For the cost of one bunch from the supermarket you can enjoy an almost permanent supply. Nothing compares with the flavour of fresh herbs and they need little space to grow. A few pots or a window box are all that's required.

Buy healthy plants from a nursery or specialist grower who will be happy to advise on planting and uses. As a general suggestion start with a few of the more common and useful varieties — parsley, basil, mint, rosemary, chives and sage.

And Finally

Try to allocate a certain amount of money each week for food and restrict yourself to this budget. If you've been relying heavily on ready-prepared items you may not manage it at first. Start by making one or two of the basic essential recipes (see next chapter). Shopping is habit-forming and eventually, with a little perseverance, you'll forget all about convenience foods. Finally, don't get tempted with non-essentials and never shop when you're hungry!

2. BACK TO BASICS

This section offers ideas for suitable accompaniments to everyday meals. Basic recipes are also given for items like pastry, sauces and batters which crop up several times throughout the book. All are easily made at home at a fraction of the cost that you would expect to pay for commercially prepared equivalents.

Short crust pastry, dumplings, pancakes and basic sauces are a cheap way of making a more substantial meal out of bits and pieces and 'stretching' more expensive ingredients like meat, fish and fruit.

Short crust pastry is used for pies, flans and quiches; dumplings can be popped into soups and casseroles; and pancakes are delicious with a variety of sweet and savoury fillings. Using a packet white sauce is three times dearer than home-made and, contrary to popular belief, isn't any quicker. Try my one-stage method on page 31 and prove it! Basic white sauce can be flavoured with chopped cooked onion, chopped parsley or grated cheese to bring variety to the weekly menu.

Ready-made potato dishes cost a fortune. Frozen chips, instant mash, potato salad and hash browns can cost up to four times as much as making your own.

BREAD

Breadline Britain

If someone had told me that that one day I'd be baking my own bread I would have roared with laughter. For bread-making is time-consuming and fiddly is it not and therefore not worth the hassle? Yet it's amazing what you do when you are on the breadline!

Surprisingly perhaps, it only takes 15-20 minutes to make the dough and the only ingredients needed are flour, yeast, salt, sugar and water. The lengthy bit is leaving the dough to rise (known as proving) but you can always do something else in the meantime. Try making a batch one wet Sunday afternoon; even better, get the kids pummelling away at the dough while you put your feet up!

Home-made bread is best eaten within a day of baking, but it will keep in reasonable condition for two to three days when stored in a tightly sealed polythene bag. After that time, thick slices make excellent Garlic Bread or Bread and Butter Pudding (see pages 18 and 120). Alternatively, make breadcrumbs which are useful for coating food prior to frying or for giving crunchy toppings to a variety of savoury dishes. Store the breadcrumbs in a lidded jar in the fridge until ready to use.

Tips For Successful Bread-Making

Strong white bread flour absorbs more water than ordinary flour because it has a higher gluten content. This results in a bigger loaf and lighter texture.

Wholemeal bread won't rise so much as a white loaf because the wholemeal flour contains less gluten than white. This prevents the yeast working quite so well.

If the water used for mixing the dough is too hot, the yeast will be killed and the bread will fail to rise. Water should therefore be luke-warm; dip your little finger into the measuring jug, the water should feel neither hot nor cold.

For the same reason, avoid leaving the dough to rise in too hot a spot. An airing cupboard or near a radiator is an ideal place.

Save time by using easy-blend dried yeast. This is available from supermarkets in boxes of eight sachets and, unlike fresh yeast or ordinary dried yeast, it can be sprinkled directly on to the flour which speeds up preparation.

Save further time by freezing uncooked dough. Make several batches in one go and then bake each loaf as you need it. Stored in an oiled, polythene bag, uncooked bread dough can be frozen for up to 3 months. Frozen dough should be thawed and then left to rise as usual before baking.

Two recipes are given here: one for basic white bread and one for wholemeal bread. If you like, you can use a combination of flours. Speciality breads can be made by adding flavourings like dried or freshly chopped herbs, finely chopped garlic or grated cheese. Or press a few black olives into the top of the dough before leaving it to rise.

What Went Wrong?

The most common mistake in bread-making is lack of patience!

If the baked bread is dense in texture, either the dough was insufficiently kneaded or not left to rise long enough.

If, on the other hand, the dough is left to rise for too long, it can collapse which results in wet and heavy bread. Generally speaking, the dough should reach the top of the tin prior to baking.

If at first you don't succeed, try again! Eventually you are bound to produce professional-looking bread. And remember, there is nothing quite like a chunk of home-made crusty bread to accompany soups, salads and many vegetarian dishes.

Tip:

Where reference is made in the recipes to a 1 lb (450g) loaf tin, the approximate size is 8″ × 4″ (20.5cm × 10cm); and a 2 lb (900g) tin is about 9″ × 5″ (23cm × 13cm).

QUICK WHITE BREAD *(makes 1 large loaf or 2 small)*

Preparation time: 15 mins.   *Cooking time: 20-40 mins.*

1 lb 6 oz (625g) strong white flour
1 level teasp salt
1 rounded teasp sugar
1 sachet easy-blend dried yeast
¾ pt (425ml) luke-warm water

1. Sieve the flour into a large bowl.

2. Mix in the salt and sugar.

3. Sprinkle on the yeast.

4. Pour on the warm water and mix to an elastic dough using a round-bladed knife.

5. Turn the dough on to a floured surface and knead for 10 minutes.

6. Grease and flour one 2 lb (900g) or two 1 lb (450g) tin(s), add the dough, and cover with greaseproof paper.

7. Leave in a warm place for about 30-40 minutes until the dough has doubled in size or reached the top of the tin.

8. Pre-heat oven to 200°C (400°F) or Gas No. 6.

9. Remove the covering paper before baking.

10. Bake large loaves for about 30-40 minutes and small loaves for about 20 minutes.

11. Remove from tin and leave on a wire rack to cool.

Tip: If the bread has been baked long enough it should sound hollow when tapped on the bottom. If you feel the bread is not quite cooked, pop it back in the oven without the tin.

QUICK WHOLEMEAL BREAD
(makes 1 large loaf or 2 small)

Wholemeal bread has more flavour than white, keeps better and is a valuable source of dietary fibre.

Preparation time: 15 mins.   *Cooking time: 20-40 mins.*

1½ lb (700g) plain wholemeal flour
1 level teasp sugar
1 sachet easy-blend dried yeast
¾ pt (425ml) luke-warm water

Follow instructions in the previous recipe for making and cooking but do not sieve the wholemeal flour.

GARLIC BREAD

This is a good way of using up semi-stale bread or your first attempts which may not have turned out quite right!

Simply butter 4 thick slices of white or wholemeal bread and then spread on some finely chopped garlic. Place the slices on a baking tray and cook for 6-10 minutes in a hot oven, 200°C (400°F) or Gas No. 6.

DUMPLINGS

Dumplings are a good way of 'stretching' expensive ingredients like meat, and also for making vegetable casseroles and soups into a more substantial meal. Traditionally beef suet was used but a vegetable version is now produced. Both are available in packets ready shredded. Dumplings are made with white or wholemeal flour and with or without suet.

SUET DUMPLINGS   *Makes about 8 to 10*

Preparation time: 10 mins.   *Cooking time: 15-20 mins.*

4 oz (110g) white self-raising flour
½ level teasp salt

2 oz (50g) shredded beef or vegetable suet
Little cold water

1. Sieve the flour and salt into a bowl, then stir in the suet.

2. Using a round-bladed knife, mix to an elastic consistency with a little cold water.

3. Form into small balls and add to soups or casseroles 15-20 minutes before the end of the cooking time.

HERB DUMPLINGS (without suet)

Makes about 8-10

Preparation time: 10 mins.   *Cooking time: 15-20 mins.*

4 oz (110g) self-raising wholemeal flour
½ level teasp salt
1 oz (25g) margarine
1 teasp dried mixed herbs OR 1 tablsp fresh chopped herbs
Freshly ground black pepper
1 size 3 egg, beaten
Little milk

1. Sieve the flour and salt into a bowl.

2. Rub in the margarine until the mixture resembles fine breadcrumbs.

3. Stir in the mixed herbs and a little pepper.

4. Using a round-bladed knife, stir in the egg and a little milk to give an elastic consistency.

5. Form into small balls and add to soups or casseroles 15-20 minutes before the end of the cooking time.

PASTRY

Short crust pastry is used for sweet and savoury pies, flans, quiches and pasties. Pastry adds bulk, making a tasty meal from a little filling.

It can be made with white or wholemeal flour, or half of each. Wholemeal pastry is more grainy than that made with white flour and has more of a tendency to crumble when being rolled out. Nonetheless many people prefer its crunchier texture and wholesome food value.

Block margarine works best as it is harder and colder and can easily be cut into correct measurements without the need for weighing, and it is cheaper than soft margarine! The rule is half fat to flour, so if you need 4 oz (110g) pastry simply halve the ingredients in the following recipes.

For best results handle pastry as little as possible and keep ingredients cold. Only use the tips of your fingers when rubbing the fat into the flour. Avoid stretching the pastry when lining a flan ring or covering a pie, for it will shrink back during baking and spoil the finished shape.

Add the water cautiously, using just enough to make a stiff dough and roll the pastry as lightly as possible.

Finally, cooked pastry is less likely to be soggy if baked in a metal dish rather than ovenproof china or glass. The exception is when a pie consists of a top crust only.

SHORT CRUST PASTRY

8 oz (225g) plain white flour
¼ level teasp salt
4 oz (110g) margarine
Little cold water

1. Sieve the flour and salt into a bowl.

2. Using the tips of your fingers, rub the margarine into the flour until the mixture resembles fine breadcrumbs.

3. Using a round-bladed knife, mix in a little cold water until a stiff dough is formed.

4. Turn out onto a lightly floured surface, roll out and use as instructed in a particular recipe.

Tip: Wrapped in foil or a polythene bag, excess pastry will keep in the fridge for 2-3 days, or, stored in a polythene bag, it can be frozen for up to 3 months. Save all scraps of pastry no matter how small. In a few weeks enough pieces will have accumulated to make a dozen jam tarts!

Tip: To save time, make large quantities of rubbed-in mixture and freeze in bags for instant pastry mix.

WHOLEMEAL PASTRY

8 oz (225g) plain wholemeal flour
¼ level teasp salt
4 oz (110g) margarine
Little cold water

1. Put the flour and salt into a bowl.

2. Using the tips of your fingers, rub in the margarine until the mixture resembles fine breadcrumbs.

3. Using a round-bladed knife, mix to a stiff dough with a little cold water.

4. Turn on to a floured surface and roll out as required.

Tip: Lining a flan tin with pastry is made easier if you roll the pastry around the rolling pin and then unroll it over the tin. If it breaks don't panic! Doing a patching job is perfectly acceptable and after all, once the filling is in, only the edges of the pastry show anyway!

SUET PASTRY

A traditional favourite, suet pastry is used for steamed savoury and sweet puddings, such as steak and kidney and jam roly-poly. This quantity is enough to line a 1½-2 pt (900ml-1.1 litre) pudding basin.

8 oz (225g) white self-raising flour
½ level teasp salt
4 oz (110g) shredded suet
Little cold water

1. Mix the flour, salt and suet together in a bowl.

2. Using a round-bladed knife, mix to an elastic dough with a little cold water. Avoid the dough becoming too wet and sticky.

3. Turn on to a floured surface and knead lightly before rolling out to about ¼" (0.5cm).

BATTERS

Batter makes a versatile base for a wide variety of sweet and savoury meals including pancakes, Yorkshire pudding, toad-in-the-hole and fritters. White or wholemeal flour can be used depending on personal taste.

PANCAKE BATTER (1) *(Makes between 8-10 pancakes)*

4 oz (110g) plain white flour
¼ level teasp salt
1 size 3 egg
½ pt (300ml) milk

1. Sieve the flour and salt into a bowl.

2. Make a well in the centre, crack in the egg and add a little of the milk.

3. Using the wooden spoon, stir briskly, gradually drawing the flour in from the sides.

4. As the mixture thickens, add more milk until it is all used up, beating well all the time. If time permits leave the batter to stand for 30 minutes before using.

WHOLEMEAL PANCAKE BATTER

Make in the same way as the previous recipe but use 4 oz (110g) plain wholemeal flour instead of white flour.

FRITTER BATTER

This is used as a coating for sweet and savoury fritters and needs to be of a thicker consistency than pancake batter. The addition of bicarbonate of soda results in a nice crispy batter.

4 oz (110g) plain white flour
¼ level teasp salt
1 rounded teasp bicarbonate of soda
1 size 3 egg
¼ pt (150ml) milk

1. Sieve the flour, salt and bicarbonate of soda into a bowl.

2. Make a well in the centre, crack in the egg and add a little of the milk.

3. Stir briskly, gradually adding the rest of the milk, beating well all the time.

POTATOES

Potatoes are an inexpensive source of carbohydrate, protein, iron, calcium, dietary fibre and particularly vitamin C. However, their goodness is easily destroyed and much depends on how they are cooked.

Boil potatoes in small amounts of liquid and drain as soon as they are cooked because vitamin C dissolves in water. A squeeze of lemon juice added to the water when boiling potatoes prevents after-cooking discolouration. Rather than slinging the goodness into the sink, use the liquid in soups and stews.

Even better, bake potatoes in their jackets or cook potatoes in ways where the liquid is part of the dish, e.g. Scalloped Potatoes (page 25) and Bombay Potatoes (page 27).

Cooking potatoes in a microwave retains more vitamin C.

Peel potatoes thinly as the nutrients lie just under the skin. Prepare potatoes just before cooking to preserve these nutrients.

When calculating quantities, allow between 6-8 oz (175-225g) of potatoes per person.

Home-grown potatoes fall roughly into three seasonal groups. In June and July come the earlies, commonly referred to as new potatoes. These are high in fibre and low in fat and are delicious boiled in their skins or used in salads. August through to March sees the second earlies, while September to May produces the maincrop.

It is useful to become familiar with certain varieties until you find a particular favourite. For example, some people like a floury-textured jacket potato whereas others may prefer a waxy, firmer flesh.

Desirée: Light yellow flesh and firm texture. Can be roasted, chipped and baked.

Maris Piper: Cream flesh with floury texture. Excellent for boiling, baking, roasting and chipping.

Pentland Squire: White flesh and floury texture. Use for mashing, baking, roasting and chipping.

King Edward: Cream flesh with floury texture. A good all purpose potato but recommended for delicious mash.

Romano: Cream flesh and waxy texture. Good for baking, roasting, boiling and chipping.

BAKED POTATOES

What costs pounds in a wine bar can be made at home for pence! Baking potatoes in their jackets is one of the most wholesome ways of cooking this humble vegetable.

1. Pre-heat oven to 200°C (400°F) or Gas No. 6.

2. Scrub the potatoes well, place them on a baking tray and cook for 45 minutes-1 hour depending on size.

One of the nicest ways of serving jacket potatoes is with a chunk of butter or margarine and some freshly ground black pepper. For a meal in itself, simply make a cut along the length of the cooked potato, gently squeeze the ends to open it up and then stuff with one of the following fillings.

1. Soured cream mixed with crisply fried chopped bacon.

2. Cream cheese mixed with chopped chives.

3. Flaked tuna fish and sweetcorn bound with mayonnaise.

4. Any minced beef filling like left-over Bolognese sauce or cottage pie mixture.

SCALLOPED POTATOES
Serves 4

Preparation time: 15 mins.   *Cooking time: 1 hour*

1½ lb (700g) potatoes
2 oz (50g) margarine
Salt and freshly ground black pepper
12 fl oz (350ml) milk

1. Pre-heat oven to 180°C (350°F) or Gas No. 4.

2. Peel and thinly slice the potatoes.

3. Grease a deep ovenproof dish and layer with the sliced potato, dotted with margarine and sprinkled with salt and pepper.

4. Pour the milk into the dish and bake for about 1 hour until the potatoes are tender.

5. Leave to stand for 5 minutes before serving.

Tip: Use large potatoes when making dishes of this kind; not only is it cheaper because there's less waste but also less time is spent peeling.

CHEESY NEW POTATO BAKE
Serves 4

Serve as an accompaniment to cold meat, chicken drumsticks or quiche, or as a meal on its own with mixed salad and crusty bread.

Preparation time: 10 mins.   *Cooking time: 1 hour*

1¼ lb (575g) new potatoes
1 oz (25g) butter or margarine
1 teasp mixed dried herbs OR 1 tablsp chopped
  fresh herbs
Salt and freshly ground black pepper
2 oz (50g) mature Cheddar cheese, grated

1. Pre-heat oven to 200°C (400°C) or Gas No. 6.

2. Grease four squares of foil about 12″ (30.5cm) in size.

3. Scrub and slice the potatoes and divide between the pieces
   of foil.

4. Sprinkle some herbs on each; season with salt and pepper
   and fold up into parcels.

5. Bake for 40 minutes and then unwrap and top with grated
   cheese. Bake uncovered for a further 10 minutes until the
   cheese is golden and bubbly.

ROASTIES   *Serves 4*

Perfect roast potatoes should be brown and crunchy on the
outside and soft and floury inside. Here's how to achieve them!

Preparation time: 5 mins.   *Cooking time: 40-50 mins.*

4 oz (110g) lard or dripping
1½ lb (700g) potatoes, peeled

1. Heat the fat in a roasting tin in a hot oven (220°C/425°F
   or Gas No. 7).

2. Cook the potatoes in boiling, salted water for 6-10 minutes
   depending on size. (This is known as par-boiling.) Drain
   well.

3. Return the potatoes to the pan and give them a good shake
   to fluff up the edges.

4. Transfer the potatoes to the roasting tin and spoon over the
   hot fat.

5. Bake for about 30-40 minutes, turning the potatoes occasionally. Drain on kitchen paper.

HASH BROWNS

Serves 4

Preparation time: 15 mins.   *Cooking time: 30 mins.*

2 lb (900g) potatoes, peeled
2 tablsp oil
1 oz (25g) butter or margarine
Salt and freshly ground black pepper

1. Par-boil the potatoes (see page 26) for 7-10 minutes depending on size. Drain and allow to cool.

2. Heat the oil and butter or margarine in a large frying pan.

3. Coarsely grate the potatoes straight into the pan and season with salt and pepper.

4. Using a spatula or fish slice, press the potato into a round and fry gently for 15 minutes.

5. Turn the potato over and fry the other side until brown.

BOMBAY POTATOES

Serves 4

Serve these tasty potatoes on their own with fresh crusty bread or as an accompaniment to cold meat or sausages.

Preparation time: 15 mins.   *Cooking time: 50 mins.*

1½ lb (700g) potatoes, peeled and diced
4 tablesp oil
2 level teasp mustard seeds
2 level teasp cumin
1 level teasp coriander
1 level teasp turmeric
1 large onion, peeled and chopped
2 cloves garlic, peeled and finely chopped

continued overleaf

Bombay Potatoes continued

1 chilli, finely chopped (optional)
Salt and freshly ground black pepper
14 oz (397g) can peeled tomatoes

1. Par-boil the potatoes (see page 26) in salted water for 5 minutes. Drain.

2. Heat the oil in a saucepan and fry the mustard seeds until they pop (about 30 seconds).

3. Stir in the cumin, coriander and turmeric and fry gently for a few seconds.

4. Add the potatoes, onion, garlic and chilli, stirring well to coat with the spices.

5. Continue frying over a low heat for 10 minutes, stirring frequently.

6. Add the salt, pepper and tomatoes and simmer for 30-40 minutes until the potatoes are tender. Stir occasionally.

Tip: Canned whole tomatoes are considerably cheaper than the ready-chopped variety and give just as good results.

RICE

Rice makes a quick and easy accompaniment which is especially suited to dishes of a liquid consistency, e.g. curries and casseroles. Rice also forms the basis of economical risottos, pilaffs and salads, to which a wide range of ingredients are added, and recipes for these are given elsewhere in the book.

Long grain white or brown rice is used for savoury dishes. Brown rice is more chewy in texture with a pleasant nutty flavour, and is a valuable source of fibre and B vitamins. White rice is polished, a process which removes the goodness of germ and bran.

Allow 2 oz (50g) of rice per person; white rice takes about

10-15 minutes to cook and brown about 30-40 minutes. There is no need to buy exotically packaged, and expensive, rice concoctions. With a little imagination it is much cheaper to create your own interesting varieties. I use supermarket 'own brands' and by observing a few rules, good results can be achieved.

Rules For Perfect Rice

1. Excess starch prevents the rice drying out into separate grains when cooked, so it is important to wash the rice under cold running water before cooking.
2. Use the amount of water stated in the recipe; adding more makes the rice soggy.
3. Don't lift the lid or stir the rice during cooking as this releases the starch causing the grains to clog together.

Tip: If rice is to be used cold for salads, cool it as quickly as possible. It can be kept overnight in the fridge. Rice should be re-heated quickly and must be hot right the way through before eating.

PLAIN WHITE RICE   *Serves 4*

Preparation time: 3 mins.   *Cooking time: 10-15 mins.*

8 oz (225g) long grain white rice
1 level teasp salt
1 pt (570ml) water

1. Wash the rice thoroughly, then put it in a saucepan with the salt and water.
2. Bring to the boil, then cover the pan and cook slowly for 10-15 minutes.

PLAIN BROWN RICE   *Serves 4*

Preparation time: 3 mins.   *Cooking time: 30-40 mins.*

8 oz (225g) brown rice
1 level teasp salt
1 pt (570ml) water

1. Wash the rice thoroughly, then put it in a saucepan with the salt and water.

2. Bring to the boil, then cover the pan and cook slowly for 30-40 minutes.

SIMPLE PILAU RICE   *Serves 4*

The simplest and cheapest pilau rice can be made by adding some chopped onion and a little turmeric to give a golden colour.

Preparation time: 5 mins.   *Cooking time: 5 mins.*

3 tablsp oil
1 onion, peeled and finely chopped
1 rounded teasp turmeric
8 oz (225g) cooked white or brown long grain rice

1. Heat the oil in a large frying pan and fry the onion gently for a few minutes until softened.

2. Stir in the turmeric and cook for a further few seconds.

3. Add the cooked rice and stir briskly until it is well coated with the spice and has heated through.

VEGETABLE RICE   *Serves 4-6*

This recipe is just a suggestion; all sorts of bits and pieces can be added. Try a few sultanas, peanuts and drained mandarin oranges. Brown rice can be treated in the same way.

Preparation time: 5 mins.   *Cooking time: 15 mins.*

8 oz (225g) long grain white rice
1 level teasp salt

1 pt (570ml) water
4 oz (110g) frozen peas, defrosted
7 oz (198g) can sweetcorn, drained

1. Wash the rice thoroughly, then put it in a saucepan with
    the salt and water.

2. Bring to the boil, then cover the pan and cook slowly for
    8 minutes.

3. Add the peas and sweetcorn and continue cooking for a
    further 6-7 minutes until the rice is tender.

SAUCES

A simple white or cheese sauce forms the basis of many of
the dishes in the book, improving their flavour and appearance.
Indeed more often than not, the sauce actually makes the dish.

There is no need to buy expensive packet mixes. Making a
sauce from scratch doesn't take any longer, especially if you
use this one-stage method.

ONE-STAGE WHITE SAUCE

1 oz (25g) flour
1 oz (25g) margarine
½ pt (300ml) cold milk
Salt and freshly ground black pepper

1. Put the first three ingredients into a small saucepan.

2. Using a balloon or wire hand whisk, beat the liquid over
    a medium heat until the mixture thickens and bubbles.

3. Season to taste with salt and pepper.

CHEESE SAUCE

Make the basic white sauce, then remove from the heat and
stir in 3 oz (75g) grated Cheddar cheese.

PARSLEY SAUCE (Good with new potatoes, leeks or boiled ham.)

Make the basic white sauce, then stir in 1-2 tablespoons chopped fresh parsley and, if liked, a squeeze of lemon juice.

MUSTARD SAUCE (Good with fish or boiled ham.)

Blend 1 level tablespoon dry mustard, 1 level teaspoon sugar and 1 tablespoon of vinegar to a smooth cream. Stir into the hot white sauce.

ONION SAUCE (Good for boiled ham or lamb.)

Cook one small chopped onion in boiling water for 10 minutes. Drain and then stir into the basic white sauce.

GRAVY

To make standard gravy to accompany a roast joint:

Remove the meat on to a serving platter. Drain off all but the sediment and about 1 tablespoon of fat from the roasting tin. Stir in 1 tablespoon of flour and mix to a paste. Gradually pour in about ½ pint (300ml) stock or water, stirring all the time. Bring to the boil and stir for 2-3 minutes until the gravy has thickened. Season to taste with salt and freshly ground black pepper.

Tip: Don't sling goodness down the drain! Use the water in which vegetables were cooked to make the gravy.

SALADS

Simple salads are one of the nicest accompaniments to a main course and a quick way of introducing vitamins, minerals and fibre to the daily diet. What is more, making your own costs a fraction of the price you have to pay for small tubs of ready-prepared salads.

Just about any combination of salad greens, vegetables, fruit and nuts can be used imaginatively. Much of the success of a salad depends on the dressing and the simplest include mayonnaise, soured cream or oil and vinegar.

The recipes suggested here are designed to accompany more substantial meals in place of cooked vegetables. Salads, however, can be a meal in themselves and suggestions for these are given elsewhere in the book.

BASIC MIXED SALAD
Serves 4

½ bunch watercress
¼ iceberg lettuce, coarsely shredded
Piece cucumber, sliced or diced
2 tomatoes, sliced or quartered

Combine all the ingredients in a serving dish and pour over a little oil and vinegar dressing.

OIL AND VINEGAR DRESSING

½ pt (300ml) oil
¼ pt (150ml) vinegar
1 level teasp salt
1 level teasp sugar
¼ level teasp freshly ground black pepper
¼ level teasp dry mustard

Put all the ingredients in a lidded glass jar and shake vigorously until thick. The dressing can be stored for several months in the fridge but should be shaken well before each use.

Tip: To keep lettuce in good condition, cut ¼" (0.5cm) off the stalk, hold upside-down under cold running water for a few seconds, shake dry and store in the fridge.

Watercress does not stay fresh long, but it will keep for a couple of days when sealed in a polythene bag in the fridge.

NEW POTATO SALAD WITH
SOURED CREAM DRESSING   *Serves 4*

Preparation time: 10 mins.   *Cooking time: 15-20 mins.*

1½ lb (700g) baby new potatoes
5 fl oz (150ml) carton soured cream
4 spring onions, chopped
½ level teasp sugar
Salt and freshly ground black pepper

1. Scrub the potatoes and cook in boiling, salted water for 15-20 minutes until tender. Drain and cool.

2. Mix the soured cream, spring onions and sugar together in a bowl.

3. Cut the potatoes in half and toss gently in the dressing. Season with salt and pepper.

WALDORF SALAD   *Serves 4*

Preparation time: 10 mins.   *Cooking time: None*

3 eating apples
2 sticks celery, chopped
2 oz (50g) walnut pieces
2 tablsp mayonnaise
Freshly ground black pepper

1. Remove the peel and core from the apples and discard. Dice the flesh.

2. Mix the diced apple with the celery, walnuts, mayonnaise and pepper.

3. SOUPS

Home-made soups have enjoyed something of a renaissance in recent years — and rightly so! They are cheap and easy to prepare; wholesome and filling to eat. This chapter includes hearty varieties which are designed to be meals in themselves.

One of the nicest accompaniments is fresh crusty bread and butter, but there are others which add bulk and flavour. These include small dumplings, croûtons, crispy bacon, cheese, pearl barley, rice and pasta (such as noodles and macaroni).

Dumplings: See page 18.

Croûtons: Cut slices of bread (stale is ideal) into small cubes and either shallow fry in a little oil and melted margarine or deep fry in a chip pan until golden brown. Drain on kitchen paper.

Bacon: Grill bacon rashers until crisp, then crumble roughly and sprinkle over the soup.

Cheese: Grated Parmesan, Cheddar or other similar hard cheese can be sprinkled on top of the soup, particularly vegetable varieties.

Pearl Barley: Add about 2 oz (50g) to the soup at the beginning of cooking. It goes well with vegetable broths.

Rice: Left-over cooked rice can be added to the soup a couple of minutes before the end of cooking. Alternatively, add uncooked rice to the soup, allowing 15 minutes' cooking time. Tomato soup and rice is a good combination.

Noodles: Cook in the soup for about 10 minutes. Noodles are especially good with chicken, or any of the thinner soups.

Macaroni: Again, good with any thin vegetable soup such as minestrone. Use the thin macaroni and allow about 15 minutes' cooking time.

STOCK

Soup can be made with water and ready-made stock cubes but the most flavour and nourishment is gained from using home-made stock. Stock is a good way of utilising ingredients which might otherwise be wasted and these include oddments of vegetables, peelings, bones, meat trimmings and chicken carcasses. Alternatively, water in which a chicken, a joint of meat or ham, or vegetables have been cooked makes instant stock.

VEGETABLE STOCK

Most vegetables can be used although I find that greens such as sprouts, cabbage and broccoli produce a too distinctive flavour. Spinach also produces a stock which is dark and dirty-looking. If a brown stock, rather than a pale colour, is preferred add onion skins. Flavour and colour can also be enhanced by the addition of yeast extract. If you like a garlic flavour, then add garlic. Vegetable stock keeps for 3-4 days in the fridge, or stored in covered, rigid containers, it can be frozen for 2-3 months.

8 oz (225g) potatoes
2 medium sized carrots
1 onion

1 stick celery
1 tablsp oil
Sprig parsley
Sprig thyme
Bay leaf
½ level teasp salt
Few peppercorns
3 pts (1.7 litres) water

1. Scrub the vegetables thoroughly and cut them into small pieces, skins and all.

2. Heat the oil in a saucepan and gently fry the vegetables for 8 minutes.

3. Add the herbs, salt, peppercorns and water.

4. Bring to the boil, cover and simmer gently for about 1½-2 hours. Strain before using.

MEAT OR BONE STOCK

Meat stock can be kept for a couple of days in the fridge.

Cooked or raw bones from meat or poultry
Meat trimmings (optional)
2 onions, cut into pieces
2 sticks celery, cut into pieces
2 medium sized carrots, cut into pieces
Sprig parsley and thyme
Peppercorns
½ level teasp salt
Bay leaf
3 pts (1.7 litres) water

Put all the ingredients into a saucepan, bring to the boil and simmer for about 3 hours. Strain before use.

FRENCH ONION SOUP   *Serves 4*

Traditionally Gruyère cheese is used in this recipe but Cheddar is cheaper and gives good results.

Preparation time: 5 mins.   *Cooking time: 40 mins.*

2 oz (50g) margarine
1½ lb (700g) onions, peeled and sliced
1 level tablsp flour
1½ pts (850ml) meat or vegetable stock
4 slices French bread
2 oz (50g) tasty Cheddar cheese, grated

1. Heat the margarine in a saucepan until it is foaming and then fry the onions for about 15-20 minutes until light brown.

2. Stir in the flour and cook for a couple of minutes.

3. Gradually add the stock, stirring all the time, bring to the boil and then simmer for 20 minutes. Adjust seasoning if necessary.

4. Divide the soup between 4 bowls, put a slice of French bread on each and top with the grated cheese.

5. Pop under a hot grill for a couple of minutes until the cheese is bubbling.

LEEK AND POTATO SOUP   *Serves 4*

As with many thick cream-style soups, the mixture should be puréed to give professional results. The use of an electric blender or food processor is therefore a distinct advantage. Failing these, rub the finished soup through a sieve.

Preparation time: 10 mins.   *Cooking time: 35 mins.*

1 oz (25g) margarine
1 lb (450g) leeks, sliced
2 medium sized potatoes, peeled and diced
2 pts (1.1 litres) vegetable or chicken stock
Salt and freshly ground black pepper

1. Melt the margarine in a large saucepan and gently fry the leeks and potatoes for 5 minutes.

2. Add the stock, bring to the boil and simmer for about 30 minutes until the potatoes are tender.

3. Purée the soup in a blender or rub through a sieve.

4. Re-heat the soup and add salt and pepper if necessary.

CREAM OF CELERY SOUP   *Serves 4*

For best results use the celery heart only. The outer stalks can be added to casseroles or used to make stock.

Preparation time: 10 mins.   *Cooking time: 40 mins.*

2 oz (50g) margarine
1 celery heart, chopped
2 oz (50g) flour
1½ pts (850ml) vegetable or chicken stock
½ pt (300ml) milk
Salt and freshly ground black pepper

1. Melt the margarine and gently fry the chopped celery for 8 minutes.

2. Stir in the flour and cook for a further minute.

3. Gradually stir in the stock and milk and then bring to the boil, stirring all the time.

4. Simmer for 30 minutes, stirring occasionally. Add salt and pepper to taste if necessary.

CREAM OF MUSHROOM SOUP   *Serves 4*

Anyone who is new to soup-making could do no better than to start with a cream-style soup. This recipe is easy and delicious.

Preparation time: 10 mins.   *Cooking time: 40 mins.*

3 oz (75g) margarine
6 oz (175g) mushrooms, thinly sliced
1 small onion, peeled and finely chopped
2 oz (50g) flour
1½ pts (850ml) vegetable or chicken stock
½ pt (300ml) milk
Salt and freshly ground black pepper

1. Melt the margarine and gently fry the mushrooms and onion for 8 minutes.

2. Stir in the flour and cook for a further minute.

3. Gradually stir in the stock and milk, bring to the boil stirring all the time and then simmer for 30 minutes.

4. Season to taste with salt and pepper.

LENTIL SOUP WITH CRISPY BACON *Serves 4-6*

To make a really hearty meal, cook small dumplings in the soup after it has been puréed (see page 18). Then top with the crispy bacon just before serving.

Preparation time: 10 mins.   *Cooking time: 40 mins.*

6 oz (175g) split red lentils, washed
8 oz (225g) potatoes, peeled and diced
2 pts (1.1 litres) meat, chicken or vegetable stock
Salt and freshly ground black pepper
4-6 rashers streaky bacon

1. Put the lentils, potatoes, stock and a little salt and pepper

in a large saucepan. Bring to the boil and simmer for 40 minutes.

2. Meanwhile, grill the bacon until really crispy and leave to cool.

3. Purée the soup in a blender or rub through a sieve.

4. Return the soup to the saucepan to re-heat, pour into individual bowls and then crumble the bacon on top.

PEA AND HAM SOUP   *Serves 4-6*

For an excellent authentic flavour make this soup after boiling a bacon joint (see page 100).

Preparation time: 10 mins.   *Cooking time: 1 hour*

2 pts (1.1 litres) bacon stock (made up with water if necessary)
6 oz (175g) dried split peas
2 oz (50g) cooked bacon or ham (from the joint), chopped

1. Put the stock and peas into a saucepan, bring to the boil and simmer gently until the peas are mushy, about 1 hour.

2. Purée the soup in a blender or rub through a sieve.

3. Add the chopped bacon or ham and re-heat before serving.

4. EGGS AND CHEESE
EGGS

There is hardly a more versatile food than an egg. A good source of protein, vitamins, fat and minerals, eggs are quick to cook in a multitude of ways, making everything from simple snacks to substantial meals. They are suitable for sweet and savoury dishes and are used in most cakes and many hot and cold desserts. Moreover, compared to meat and fish, eggs are cheap. Half a dozen or so and a few bits and pieces and you have a nutritious, economical and filling meal for four.

Check butchers' prices before buying; they're often cheaper than supermarkets.

Eggs are graded according to size with sizes 2 and 3 probably being the most useful in general cookery.

To separate an egg: Some recipes demand that the yolks and whites are added separately to other ingredients. For example in soufflés, in some batters and in meringue where only the whites are used.

Crack the egg smartly against the side of a bowl and then,

holding it over the bowl, break the shell in half holding the cracked sides up. Pass the yolk back and forth between the two shells; the white will drop into the basin and the yolk can be popped into a cup.

CHEESE

Cheese varies greatly in price, texture and flavour but generally speaking most varieties are an economical, nutritious and useful ingredient in basic cookery. Store cheese in a cool, airy place, lightly wrapped. The following is a list of the cheese used in this chapter.

Cheddar: The most useful in everyday cooking. Flavours range from mild to quite strong, known as mature, tasty or Farmhouse Cheddar. It is false economy to use a milder, yet cheaper, variety in cooking because the depth of flavour is insufficient to give the necessary 'bite'. Cheddar is invaluable for sauces, toppings and quiches.

Parmesan: A hard Italian cheese which is available, finely grated, in handy tubs. Its strong distinctive flavour means a little goes a long way and it lasts for weeks in the fridge. Use for sprinkling over pasta dishes to give added flavour or for topping vegetarian dishes prior to baking or grilling.

Mozzarella: A soft, mild-flavoured Italian cheese which is deliciously gooey and stringy when cooked. It is essential for pizza toppings and, although fairly expensive, can be mixed with grated Cheddar for economy.

Cream Cheese: As its name suggests, cream cheese is made from cream rather than milk. It has a soft, buttery texture and mild flavour. Use in pancake stuffings, pâtés, and quiches.

Blue Cheeses: These are more expensive and include soft, semi-hard and hard, with a blue vein running through the white cheese. Most have a sharp pungent flavour and are ideal for crumbling into salads, quiches or making blue cheese dressing. Stilton, Danish Blue, Roquefort, Dolcelatte, Bleu de Bresse, Gorgonzola and Bleu D'Auvergne are all examples.

BREAKFAST-STYLE OMELETTE   *Serves 4*

Cooking omelettes in this way, i.e. like one big pancake, is much quicker and easier than the traditional, individual method.

Preparation time: 10 mins.   *Cooking time: 20 mins.*

12 oz (350g) potatoes, peeled and diced
1 tablsp oil
4 oz (110g) streaky bacon, chopped
6 size 2 eggs, beaten
3 tablsp milk
Salt and freshly ground black pepper

1. Cook the potatoes in boiling, salted water for about 5 minutes until just tender. Drain.

2. Meanwhile, heat the oil and fry the chopped bacon for 5 minutes.

3. Add the potatoes and continue frying gently for a further 10 minutes. Stir the mixture frequently to prevent sticking.

4. Pre-heat grill to medium.

5. Mix the eggs, milk and seasoning together and pour into the frying pan.

6. Cook over a gentle heat until the mixture half sets, then pop under the grill for a few minutes until golden brown and puffy. Cut into wedges and serve immediately.

OMELETTE MARGUERITA   *Serves 4*

Surprisingly this is quite a substantial meal and is good served with salad and fresh bread.

Preparation time: 10 mins.   *Cooking time: 15 mins.*

2 tablsp oil
4 spring onions, sliced
4 oz (110g) mushrooms, sliced
4 oz (110g) sliced salami
6 size 2 eggs, beaten
3 tablsp milk
Salt and freshly ground black pepper
2 oz (50g) Cheddar cheese, grated

1. Heat the oil in a large frying pan and sauté the spring onions and mushrooms for 8 minutes until tender.

2. Cut each slice of salami into 4 pieces, add to the pan and fry gently for a couple of minutes.

3. Pre-heat the grill to medium.

4. Mix the beaten eggs, milk and seasoning together and pour into the frying pan.

5. Cook over a gentle heat until the mixture half-sets then sprinkle on the cheese.

6. Pop the frying pan under the grill for a few minutes until golden brown and puffy. Cut into wedges and serve immediately.

CHEESE SOUFFLÉ
Serves 2

This makes a tasty, yet cheap, light lunch or supper dish. Serve with salad and garlic bread.

Preparation time: 10 mins.   *Cooking time: 20 mins.*

1 oz (25g) margarine
1½ level tablsp flour
½ level teasp dry mustard
¼ pt (150ml) milk
3 oz (75g) tasty Cheddar cheese, grated

continued overleaf

Cheese Soufflé continued

3 size 3 eggs, separated
Salt and freshly ground black pepper
Few chopped fresh chives (optional)

1. Pre-heat oven to 180°C (350°F) or Gas No. 4.

2. Grease two individual soufflé dishes, 4" (10.2cm) in diameter or one dish about 6" (15.2cm).

3. Melt the margarine in a medium sized saucepan, add the flour and mustard and stir over a low heat to make a thick glossy paste.

4. Gradually stir in the milk; bring to the boil, stirring all the time until the sauce has thickened.

5. Add the grated cheese and stir until melted.

6. Now beat in the egg yolks one by one, using a wooden spoon.

7. Season with salt and pepper and stir in the chives if using.

8. In a bowl whisk the egg whites until stiff then, using a metal spoon, fold the whites into the cheese mixture.

9. Pour into the prepared dishes or dish and bake for 15-20 minutes until the soufflés are well risen and golden.

Tip: These make an economical and unusual starter for a dinner party. (For other dinner party dishes, see Chapter 12, Entertaining On A Budget.)

CHEESE AND ONION FLAN   *Serves 4*

A simple flan which is good served with jacket potatoes and salad.

Preparation time: 15 mins.   *Cooking time: 45 mins.*

2 onions, peeled and chopped
1 tablsp oil
4 oz (110g) short crust pastry (half the recipe on
    page 20)
3 oz (75g) tasty Cheddar cheese, grated
2 size 2 eggs, beaten
Approx. ¼ pt (150ml) milk
Salt and freshly ground black pepper

1.   Fry the onions in the oil for about 15 minutes until lightly brown.

2.   Meanwhile, make the pastry according to instructions on page 20, halving the ingredients.

3.   Roll out and use to line an 8″ (20.5cm) flan ring or sandwich tin.

4.   Pre-heat oven to 200°C (400°F) or Gas No. 6.

5.   Put the drained onions and grated cheese in the pastry case.

6.   Beat the eggs in a measuring jug and make up to ½ pt (300ml) with milk. Season with salt and pepper.

7.   Strain the egg mixture into the pastry case and bake for about 30 minutes until well risen and golden brown.

SPINACH ROULADE WITH CREAMY MUSHROOM FILLING
Serves 4

A roulade is similar to a soufflé in texture but made flat in a Swiss roll tin and then rolled around a filling. I particularly like the combination of spinach and creamy mushrooms in this recipe. Serve with a potato salad or fresh crusty bread and butter. For best results, eat the roulade as soon as possible after cooking.

Preparation time: 25 mins.   *Cooking time: 12 mins.*

1½ lb (700g) spinach
4 size 2 eggs
Salt and freshly ground black pepper
2 oz (50g) margarine
6 oz (175g) mushrooms, sliced
1 oz (25g) flour
4 fl oz (120ml) milk
Grated Parmesan cheese

1. Pre-heat oven to 200°C (400°F) or Gas No. 6.

2. Grease and line a Swiss roll tin or baking tray about 8″×12″ (20.5cm×30cm).

3. Discard any very coarse stalks from the spinach, wash the leaves and then cook without using extra water until just tender, about 8 minutes. Drain then chop finely.

4. Separate the eggs, putting the whites into a large bowl.

5. Stir the yolks into the spinach and season with salt and pepper.

6. Whisk the egg whites until they are stiff enough to stand in soft peaks.

7. Very lightly fold the whites into the spinach mixture.

8. Pour the mixture into the prepared tin and bake for 12-15 minutes until lightly brown and firm to the touch.

9. Meanwhile, melt the margarine in a small saucepan and gently fry the mushrooms for 8 minutes.

10. Stir in the flour and cook for 1 minute.

11. Gradually stir in the milk. Bring to the boil and stir for a couple of minutes until the mixture thickens.

12. Have ready a damp tea towel, doubled and laid flat on a work surface. Lay a sheet of greaseproof paper on top and sprinkle with a little grated Parmesan cheese. (The damp

tea-towel creates steam when the hot roulade is turned out, thus minimising it cracking when being rolled up.)

13. Turn the roulade out on to the greaseproof paper and peel off the lining paper.

14. Spread on the mushroom mixture to within 2" (5cm) of the edge.

15. Roll up the roulade like a Swiss roll, using the greaseproof paper to help ease it into shape.

QUICHE LORRAINE
Serves 4

Home-made quiches are much crisper and tastier than the often soggy bought varieties. Serve this inexpensive supper with jacket or new potatoes and salad.

Preparation time: 15 mins.   *Cooking time: 30 mins.*

4 oz (110g) streaky bacon OR bacon bits
6 oz (175g) short crust pastry (see page 20)
2 oz (50g) tasty Cheddar cheese, grated
2 size 2 eggs, beaten
½ pt (300ml) milk
Salt and freshly ground black pepper

1. Pre-heat oven to 200°C (400°F) or Gas No. 6.

2. Grill the bacon until crisp and then cut into pieces.

3. Meanwhile, make the pastry as per page 20 but use 6 oz (170g) of flour and 3 oz (75g) margarine only.

4. Roll out the pastry and use to line an 8" (20.5cm) flan ring or sandwich tin.

5. Put the bacon and cheese in the pastry case.

6. Beat the eggs, milk, salt and pepper together and strain through a sieve into the pastry case.

7. Bake for about 30 minutes until the filling is brown and firm to the touch.

BLUE CHEESE QUICHE   *Serves 4*

Traditionally Roquefort cheese is used but as it is the most expensive of the blue cheeses, alternatives such as Danish Blue or Bleu D'Auvergne are cheaper and work well. Served immediately after cooking, this quiche has a soufflé-like texture but it is also delicious cold when the texture is more solid like a cheesecake. Jacket potatoes and a salad are good accompaniments.

Preparation time: 20 mins.   *Cooking time: 30 mins.*

6 oz (175g) short crust pastry (see page 20)
5 oz (125g) Bleu D'Auvergne or Danish Blue cheese
4 oz (113g) carton cream cheese
2 size 2 eggs, beaten
¼ pt (150ml) milk
Few chopped chives OR 1 small onion, finely chopped

1. Pre-heat oven to 200°C (400°F) or Gas No. 6.

2. Make the pastry as per page 20 but use only 6 oz (175g) flour and 3 oz (75g) margarine.

3. Roll out the pastry and use to line an 8″ (20.5cm) flan ring or sandwich tin.

4. Cream the cheeses together until well blended and then beat in the eggs and milk.

5. Finally stir in the chives or onion and pour the mixture into the pastry case.

6. Bake for about 15 minutes and then turn the oven down to 180°C (350°F) or Gas No. 4 and cook for a further 15 minutes until the quiche is golden brown and puffy.

5. PASTA AND PIZZA

PASTA

Tasty pasta dishes can be made from as few or as many ingredients as you like but most provide a cheap meal. At the bottom of the price range are simple sauces, such as those made from a can of chopped tomatoes and some freshly chopped basil; or from melted butter, grated cheese and ground black pepper.

Rising up the scale, you can add a selection from the following: chopped ham, crispy bacon, sliced fried mushrooms, tuna fish, prawns, olives, sweetcorn, cooked vegetables, salami, meatballs, chopped onion, herbs and, probably the best known of all, minced beef as in Spaghetti Bolognese.

Types of Pasta

Pasta is made from wheat, finely ground into semolina and then mixed with water to form a dough. Sometimes egg or spinach is added, or wholemeal semolina used, which produces a yellow, green or brown colour respectively.

Although fresh pasta is available, the cheapest and most

commonly used in this country are the dried versions. There is a wide variety of shapes, including spaghetti, tagliatelli, noodles, macaroni, bows, spirals, shells, wheels, cannelloni (fat tubes which are stuffed) and lasagne (flat sheets which are layered up with a meat or vegetable mixture).

To Cook Pasta

Boil plenty of salted water and add a teaspoon of cooking oil to prevent the pasta clogging together. Cook rapidly for 8-10 minutes, moving the pasta occasionally with a fork to prevent it sticking. With spaghetti, hold the end of a bunch in the water and, as it softens, coil the rest into the pan. Lasagne and cannelloni are available which require no pre-cooking. This saves a lot of time and fuss, but the mixture used should be fairly liquid otherwise the pasta might be rather doughy when cooked.

Serving Quantities

Allow between 2 oz (50g) and 3 oz (75g) of pasta per person, depending on appetite.

SPAGHETTI CON FORMAGGIO   *Serves 4*

A dish of spaghetti, glistening with oil, is topped with a tasty mixture of crispy bacon, onions, mushrooms and cheese. Serve with garlic bread and salad.

Preparation time: 10 mins.   *Cooking time: 30 mins.*

8 oz (225g) streaky bacon, chopped
2 tablsp oil
1 onion, peeled and chopped
8 oz (225g) mushrooms, sliced
8-10 oz (225-275g) spaghetti
4 oz (110g) tasty Cheddar cheese, grated
Extra oil

1. Fry the bacon for 10 minutes, then add the oil, onion and mushrooms and fry gently for a further 10 minutes.

2. Meanwhile, cook the spaghetti in boiling, salted water for about 8 minutes until tender.

3. Pre-heat grill to high.

4. Drain the spaghetti well, return to saucepan and toss in a good slug of oil until it glistens.

5. Pour the spaghetti into a shallow ovenproof dish and spoon the bacon mixture on top.

6. Top with grated cheese and grill under a high heat for a couple of minutes until golden brown.

CHILLI PASTA

Serves 4

Cans of beans are now available in a mild chilli sauce. Give them a try in this quick and tasty supper dish.

Preparation time: 5 mins.   *Cooking time: 18 mins.*

1 large onion, peeled and chopped
4 oz (110g) mushrooms, sliced
2 tablsp oil
14 oz (400g) can red kidney beans in chilli sauce
14 oz (397g) can peeled tomatoes, drained
Salt and freshly ground black pepper
8 oz (225g) tagliatelli

1. Fry the onion and mushrooms gently in the oil for 10 minutes.

2. Stir in the beans, tomatoes, salt and pepper and simmer for 8 minutes.

3. Meanwhile, cook the tagliatelli in boiling, salted water for about 8 minutes until tender. Drain.

4. Divide the tagliatelli between 4 plates and top with the bean mixture.

BUTTERED TAGLIATELLI WITH BASIL AND MUSHROOMS

Serves 4

If you've followed my advice in Chapter 1, a nice clump of fresh basil should be growing in a pot! Don't be tempted to use dried herbs in this recipe, if necessary substitute parsley.

Preparation time: 10 mins.   *Cooking time: 20 mins.*

2 tablsp oil
8 oz (225g) mushrooms, sliced thinly
1 red pepper, sliced thinly
8-12 oz (225g-350g) tagliatelli
1 tablsp freshly chopped basil
Juice 1 lemon
Salt and freshly ground black pepper
3 oz (75g) butter or margarine
Grated Parmesan cheese

1. Heat the oil in a frying pan and sauté the mushrooms and red pepper for 10 minutes.

2. Meanwhile, cook the tagliatelli in boiling, salted water for about 12 minutes until tender. Drain.

3. Stir the basil, lemon juice, salt and pepper into the mushroom mixture and cook gently for a couple of minutes.

4. Return the drained tagliatelli to the saucepan and stir in the mushroom mixture and the butter.

5. Turn into a serving dish or individual plates and sprinkle with grated Parmesan cheese and plenty of freshly ground black pepper.

SPAGHETTI WITH FRESH TOMATO SAUCE

Serves 4

Use ripe juicy tomatoes in this recipe. If the tomatoes are too firm, the sauce will be too thick in which case add a splash or two of water. Apart from serving with pasta, the sauce makes a wonderful accompaniment to fish cakes, meat loaves and sausages.

Preparation time: 15 mins.   *Cooking time: 40 mins.*

3 tablsp oil
1 onion, peeled and chopped
2 cloves garlic, peeled and finely chopped
1 lb (450g) ripe tomatoes
1 tablsp tomato purée
Salt and freshly ground black pepper
1 bay leaf
8-12 oz (225-350g) spaghetti
1 tablsp freshly chopped basil
Grated Parmesan cheese (optional)

1. Heat the oil in a saucepan and gently fry the onion and garlic for 3-4 minutes.

2. Meanwhile, plunge the tomatoes into boiling water for a minute and then peel off and discard the skins. Roughly chop the flesh.

3. Add the tomatoes, tomato purée, salt, pepper and bay leaf to the onion and garlic.

4. Put a lid on the pan and cook very gently for 40 minutes. Stir the sauce occasionally, mashing the tomatoes against the side of the pan.

5. About 12 minutes before the sauce is ready, cook the spaghetti in boiling, salted water. Drain.

6. Remove the bay leaf from the sauce and stir in the chopped basil.

7. Tip the spaghetti into a serving dish or spoon on to individual plates and top with tomato sauce. Sprinkle with grated Parmesan cheese if liked.

Tip: In the autumn when tomatoes are at their cheapest, or if you spot a bargain bag at rock bottom price, make a bulk batch of sauce. Stored in a covered, rigid container, the sauce can be frozen for 2-3 months.

SARDINE AND MACARONI GRILL   *Serves 4*

A tasty variation of macaroni cheese. Can be served on its own or with garlic bread and salad.

Preparation time: 10 mins.   *Cooking time: 20 mins.*

6 oz (175g) macaroni
2 oz (50g) margarine
4 oz (110g) mushrooms, sliced
1 oz (25g) flour
½ pt (300ml) milk
Salt and freshly ground black pepper
2 tomatoes, sliced
4.23 oz (120g) can sardines in oil, drained
2 oz (50g) tasty Cheddar cheese, grated

1. Pre-heat grill.

2. Cook the macaroni in boiling, salted water for about 8 minutes until tender. Drain.

3. Melt the margarine and fry the mushrooms for a few minutes until tender.

4. Stir in the flour and cook for 1 minute.

5. Gradually add the milk, stirring all the time. Bring to the boil and stir until thickened.

6. Season with salt and pepper and then stir in the macaroni.

7. Turn the mixture into a shallow ovenproof dish and top with the sliced tomatoes, lightly mashed sardines and grated cheese.

8. Pop under the grill for a few minutes until brown and bubbly.

MACARONI AND TUNA BAKE   *Serves 4*

Serve with garlic bread and salad or simply on its own.

Preparation time: 15 mins.   *Cooking time: 20 mins.*

6 oz (175g) macaroni
½ pt (300ml) white sauce (see page 31)
7 oz (185g) can tuna fish in oil, drained and flaked
4 oz (110g) frozen peas
3 oz (75g) tasty Cheddar cheese, grated

1. Pre-heat oven to 180°C (350°F) or Gas No. 4.

2. Cook the macaroni in boiling, salted water for about 8 minutes until tender. Drain.

3. Meanwhile, make the white sauce according to instructions on page 31.

4. Stir the macaroni, tuna and peas into the sauce and turn into a shallow ovenproof dish.

5. Sprinkle the cheese over the top and bake for about 20 minutes until brown and bubbly.

SPAGHETTI ALLA CARBONARA   *Serves 4*

A traditional Italian dish — spaghetti with bacon and eggs.

Preparation time: 10 mins.   *Cooking time: 15 mins.*

8 oz (225g) spaghetti
1 tablsp oil
8 oz (225g) smoked streaky bacon, diced
2 size 2 eggs, beaten
5 fl oz (142ml) single cream
Salt and freshly ground black pepper
Grated Parmesan cheese

1. Cook the spaghetti in boiling, salted water for about 12 minutes until tender. Drain.

2. Meanwhile, heat the oil and fry the bacon for about 10 minutes until crisp.

3. Beat the eggs, cream, salt and pepper and a little Parmesan cheese together.

4. Tip the spaghetti back into the pan, add the bacon and cream mixture and cook gently for 3 minutes. Turn into a serving dish and sprinkle with more Parmesan cheese.

MOZZARELLA AND TOMATO QUILLS *Serves 3-4*

A deliciously simple and tasty supper dish. Serve with salad and garlic bread.

Preparation time: 15 mins.   *Cooking time: 10 mins.*

6 oz (175g) pasta quills or fat tubes
14 oz (397g) can peeled tomatoes, drained
2 tablsp oil
5 oz (150g) Mozzarella cheese, diced
2 tablsp freshly chopped basil
Salt and freshly ground black pepper
Grated Parmesan cheese

1. Cook the pasta in boiling, salted water until tender, for about 10 minutes. Drain.

2. Pre-heat oven to 200°C (400°F) or Gas No. 6.

3. Put the tomatoes and oil in a small saucepan and cook gently for 5 minutes, breaking up the tomatoes against the side of the pan.

4. Add the Mozzarella, basil, salt and pepper and heat gently for 1 minute.

5. Turn the pasta into a shallow ovenproof dish and pour over the sauce.

6. Sprinkle over some grated Parmesan cheese and bake for 10 minutes.

Tip: If you have haven't got a pot of basil growing in your garden, substitute a can of chopped tomatoes with herbs for the peeled tomatoes and basil; it's cheaper than buying fresh basil.

PIZZA

Commercially prepared pizzas cost a fortune and they're not always overly generous on taste and abundance of topping. You can put almost anything you like on a home-made version so take the following recipe as an idea only. It happens to be my particular favourite! According to personal preference choose from ham, pineapple, onions, mushrooms, peppers, chillies, bacon, salami, tuna fish, olives, spring onions, anchovies and garlic. The only two essential ingredients, which form the basis of all pizzas, are tomatoes and cheese. In fact, if you're really pushed for money, a tasty pizza can be made from using these alone.

Pizza base is the same as a bread dough (see page 17). White or wholemeal flour can be used or strong white or bread flour.

The only accompaniment necessary is a nice mixed salad, tossed in a vinaigrette dressing.

Tip: Mozzarella cheese − the type that goes all gooey and stringy when cooked − is traditionally used for pizzas. As this is expensive, I mix it with grated Cheddar because the secret of a good pizza is to have a generous topping of golden bubbly cheese.

BASIC PIZZA DOUGH

Serves 4

This quantity makes two 10-12″ (25.5-30.5cm) pizzas or four individual pizzas of about 7½″ (19cm) each.

Preparation time: 15 mins. + 30 mins. for the dough to rise

1 lb (450g) plain white or wholemeal flour
1 level teasp sugar
1 level teasp salt
1 sachet easy-blend dried yeast
½ pt (300ml) luke warm water

1. Put the flour, sugar and salt together in a bowl and mix in the easy-blend dried yeast.

2. Using a round-bladed knife, stir in the water to form an elastic dough.

3. Turn the dough on to a floured surface and knead for 10 minutes.

4. Either cut the dough into 2 or 4 pieces and roll each out into rounds about ⅜″ (1cm) thick.

5. Lay the pizza bases on an oiled baking tray and put in a warm place for about 30 minutes until the dough is puffy.

MY FAVOURITE PIZZA

Serves 4

Preparation time: 10 mins. +   *Cooking time: 20 mins.*
making the dough

1 lb (450g) pizza dough (see previous recipe)
1 oz (25g) margarine
4 oz (110g) mushrooms, sliced
3-4 tablsp tomato purée
14 oz (397g) can peeled tomatoes, drained
Salt and freshly ground black pepper
1 tablsp chopped fresh basil (optional)
3-4 spring onions, chopped
4 oz (110g) sliced spicy sausage or salami
6 oz (175g) Mozzarella cheese, grated
2 oz (50g) tasty Cheddar cheese, grated

1. Make the pizza bases and leave to rise as per the previous recipe.

2. Meanwhile, melt the margarine and sauté the mushrooms for 5 minutes.

3. When the pizza bases have risen slightly and become puffy, press the dough down gently to within 1" (2.5cm) of the edge.

4. Pre-heat the oven to 200°C (400°F) or Gas No. 6.

5. Spread the pizza bases with tomato purée to within 1" (2.5cm) of the edge.

6. Top with a layer of sliced canned tomatoes.

7. Sprinkle with salt, pepper, basil and spring onions.

8. Spread on a layer of drained mushrooms and top with sliced spicy sausage or salami.

9. Mix the two cheeses together and sprinkle on top of the pizzas.

10. Bake for about 15-20 minutes until the pizza crust is golden and the cheese brown and bubbly.

BARGAIN PIZZA
Serves 4

Preparation time: 10 mins +   *Cooking time: 20 mins.*
making the dough

1 lb (450g) pizza dough (see page 60)
4 tablsp tomato purée
14 oz (397g) can peeled tomatoes, drained
Salt and freshly ground black pepper
1 tablsp chopped fresh basil (optional)
6 oz (175g) Mozzarella cheese, grated
2 oz (50g) tasty Cheddar cheese, grated

1. Make the pizza bases and leave to rise according to instructions on page 60.

2. Pre-heat oven to 200°C (400°F) or Gas No. 6.

3. When the pizza bases have risen slightly and become puffy, press the dough down gently to within 1″ (2.5cm) of the edge.

4. Spread with tomato purée and top with sliced canned tomatoes. Sprinkle with salt, pepper and basil.

5. Mix the cheeses together and sprinkle on top of the pizzas.

6. Bake for 15-20 minutes until golden and bubbly.

6. VEGETARIAN MEALS

See also Eggs and Cheese (page 42) and Pasta (page 51)

Currently some six per cent of Great Britain's population do not eat the flesh of animals, birds or fish. Yet for those who are not strictly vegetarian, meatless meals offer enormous scope for cost-conscious but interesting meals.

Vegetarian restaurants have sprung up all over the country to meet the demand and, as anyone who has sampled the fare will testify, prices are anything but humble. Once you become familiar with vegetarian ingredients it becomes quite easy to adapt expensive restaurant meals for home cooking.

In addition to lentils, beans and nuts the vegetarian diet makes great use of fresh fruit and vegetables and these are cheap if you buy them in season (see also Chapter 1, Cost-cutters). Years ago, people had to make use of what was available. They looked forward to the delicious taste of those first new potatoes and waited in anticipation for the treat of the strawberry season. A lot of pleasure came from cooking and eating produce which hadn't been available for months. Now you can buy just about anything all the year round. It's very convenient of course but convenience is costly!

The price of more ordinary vegetables like mushrooms, carrots and onions remains fairly static throughout the year but those at the exotic end of the market such as courgettes, asparagus and even tomatoes, are cheaper at certain times. To some extent price is also governed by the weather. However, it pays to know when fruit and vegetables are in season because it can make a great difference to the household budget. The following list gives a rough guide.

Aubergines:	July-Aug.	*Mushrooms:*	All year.
Broad Beans:	June-Aug.	*New Potatoes:*	May-June.
Broccoli:	April-May.	*Onions:*	All year.
	Aug.-Nov.	*Parsnips:*	Oct.-March.
Cabbage:	All year.	*Peas (fresh):*	May-Sept.
Carrots:	All year.	*Peppers:*	Aug.-Nov.
Cauliflower:	June-Oct.	*Runner Beans:*	Aug.-Oct.
Celery:	Sept.-Feb.	*Spinach:*	May-Oct.
Chicory:	Sept.-April.	*Spring Greens:*	Most of
Courgettes:	June-Sept.		the year.
Cress:	All year.	*Spring Onions:*	May-Sept.
Cucumber:	June-Sept.	*Sprouts:*	Sept.-March
Fennel:	Aug.-Nov.	*Sweet Corn:*	May-Aug.
Leeks:	Sept.-March.	*Tomatoes:*	May.
Lettuce:	May-Oct.		July-Sept.
Marrow:	July-Oct.		

Other useful ingredients in the vegetarian diet are dried peas, beans and lentils. Known as pulses, these are a good source of protein, vitamins, minerals and fibre, are low in fat and cost a fraction of the price of meat.

Although there are over 20 different varieties of peas and beans, most supermarkets sell a good pre-packaged range of 'own label' which are usually cheaper than branded goods. Canned peas and beans are also available but, although they are quick to heat, are more expensive pound for pound.

Dried peas and beans should be soaked overnight to reduce the cooking time. The soaking process can be speeded up by boiling the beans for a good 5 minutes and then turning off the heat and leaving to soak in the hot water for an hour. One point worth noting is not to add salt during cooking as this toughens the outer skin, making the cooking time even longer.

The following is a list of the more common varieties. Experiment yourself as each has its own flavour and texture which brings variety and interest to recipes.

Split Peas: Do not require soaking; cook for about 40 minutes. Use in soups, casseroles and classic dishes like Pease Pudding.

Chick Peas: Should be soaked followed by about 40 minutes cooking. Popular in Greece and Turkey where they are cooked and then coated in olive oil, lemon juice, salt, pepper and garlic to make delicious 'nibbles'.

Red Kidney Beans: Although the average healthy person should not be affected, red kidney beans can cause stomach upsets if they are not cooked properly.

Soak the beans in cold water for several hours or overnight. Drain the beans, then bring to the boil in plenty of fresh water. Boil rapidly for 10 minutes to destroy any toxins in the outer skin, then turn the heat down and simmer for about 50 minutes until the beans are soft.

Kidney beans have a floury texture and a sweetish flavour; good in spicy casseroles, beanburgers and salads.

Butter Beans: Should be soaked and then cooked for about 1½ hours. Make a good alternative to potatoes as an accompaniment to boiled bacon. Can also be added to casseroles.

Haricot Beans: Should be soaked and then cooked for about 1½ hours. The traditional bean for the classic dish Boston Baked Beans. Can also be combined with vegetables for spicy casseroles and salads.

Blackeyed Beans: Should be soaked and then cooked for about 30 minutes. Use in casseroles and beanburgers.

Red Lentils: Do not need soaking. They cook within 15-20 minutes and have a soft texture and easily disintegrate. Nonetheless red lentils make excellent soup and are good in quiches, vegetarian loaves and for thickening and adding bulk to casseroles.

Continental Lentils: These are green/brown in colour and do not need soaking. They have a firm texture and nutty flavour and their ability to stay whole when cooked makes them ideal in many vegetarian recipes.

MUSHROOM DOPIAZZA   *Serves 2*

This is one of several recipes which I have adapted from similar commercially prepared examples — at one third of the price!

Preparation time: 10 mins.   *Cooking time: 20 mins.*

3 tablsp oil
12 oz (350g) mushrooms, thinly sliced
1 large onion, peeled and roughly chopped
1 clove garlic, peeled and finely chopped
Salt and freshly ground black pepper
1 teasp flour
1 teasp garam masala
2 teasp paprika
1 teasp cumin
1 teasp ground ginger
1 teasp coriander
14 oz (397g) can peeled tomatoes

1. Heat the oil in a large frying pan and gently cook the mushrooms, onion and garlic for 10 minutes.

2. Stir in the remaining ingredients ending with tomatoes, and cook gently for a further 10 minutes.

COURGETTES AND TOMATOES WITH BASIL
Serves 2

Make this tasty, light lunch or supper dish when courgettes reach rock bottom price, usually in June or July. Serve with fresh crusty bread and butter.

Preparation time: 10 mins.   *Cooking time: 10 mins.*

1 tablsp oil
1 lb (450g) courgettes, sliced
2 beefsteak tomatoes
Salt and freshly ground black pepper
2 tablsp roughly chopped fresh basil

1. Heat the oil in a saucepan or large frying pan and stir-fry the courgettes for 5 minutes.

2. Remove and discard the skins from the tomatoes by spearing with a fork and plunging into boiling water for a few seconds. Slice the flesh.

3. Add the tomatoes, salt, pepper and basil to the courgettes and continue stir-frying for a further 5 minutes until the courgettes are tender and the tomatoes have broken down.

TOMATO, BEAN AND CHEESE BAKE   *Serves 2*

Serve with garlic bread or brown rice.

Preparation time: 15 mins.   *Cooking time: 30 mins.*

2 onions, peeled and roughly chopped
1 lb (450g) runner beans, sliced
2 beefsteak tomatoes
Freshly ground black pepper
½ pt (300ml) basic white sauce (see page 31)
4 oz (110g) Cheddar cheese, grated

1. Pre-heat the oven to 180°C (350°F) or Gas No. 4.

2. Cook the onions and beans in boiling, salted water for about 10 minutes until just tender. Drain.

3. Peel the tomatoes by spearing with a fork and dipping in boiling water for a few seconds. Roughly chop the flesh.

4.   Mix the onions, beans and tomatoes together and season with black pepper.

5.   Make the sauce as per page 31.

6.   Stir the sauce into the vegetables and pour the mixture into a shallow ovenproof dish.

7.   Top with grated cheese and bake for 20 minutes until the cheese is golden brown and bubbly.

SPICY VEGETABLE HOT POT   *Serves 4*

This is an ideal recipe for using up odd vegetables. Serve with plenty of fresh crusty bread or garlic bread.

Preparation time: 10 mins.   *Cooking time: 35 mins.*

2 tablsp oil
1 medium sized leek, sliced
1 medium sized courgette, sliced
1 medium sized carrot, sliced thinly
1 onion, peeled and chopped
4 oz (110g) button mushrooms
8 oz (225g) potatoes, peeled and diced
14 oz (397g) can peeled tomatoes
7.5 oz (220g) can red kidney beans, drained
½ pt (300ml) water
1 tablsp tomato purée
1 rounded teasp chilli powder
Salt and freshly ground black pepper
1 level tablsp cornflour or flour

1.   Heat the oil in a saucepan and sauté the leek, courgette, carrot, onion and mushrooms for 5 minutes.

2.   Meanwhile, par-boil (see page 26) the diced potatoes for 5 minutes. Drain and then add to the other vegetables.

3. Stir in the tomatoes, drained beans, water, tomato purée, chilli powder, salt and pepper.

4. Bring to the boil and then simmer gently, without a lid, for about 30 minutes until the vegetables are tender.

5. Mix the cornflour or flour with a little water and stir into the vegetable mixture. Boil up for a couple of minutes to thicken.

Tip: A more substantial dish can be made by turning the mixture into an ovenproof dish, topping with sliced cooked potato and sprinkling with a little grated cheese. Simply pop under the grill until brown and crispy.

LENTIL MOUSSAKA   *Serves 4*

Nutty flavoured green lentils combine with tomatoes and yeast extract to produce a rich and flavourful alternative to traditional minced lamb. Serve with fresh crusty bread.

Preparation time: 20 mins.   *Cooking time: 50 mins.*

7 tablsp oil
1 onion, peeled and chopped
3 sticks celery, sliced
1 clove garlic, peeled and finely chopped
8 oz (225g) green lentils
Freshly ground black pepper
14 oz (397g) can peeled tomatoes
1 tablsp yeast extract
1¼ pts (700ml) water
12 oz (350g) aubergines (about 1 large)
½ pt (300ml) cheese sauce (see page 31)

1. Heat 1 tablespoon of the oil in a saucepan and gently fry the onion, celery and garlic for 5 minutes.

2. Add the lentils, a good shake of pepper, tomatoes, yeast extract and water.

3. Bring to the boil and then simmer for about 40 minutes until the lentils are tender.

4. Meanwhile slice the aubergine and fry in the remainder of the oil for a few minutes on each side until lightly brown. Drain on kitchen paper.

5. Pre-heat oven to 180°C (350°F) or Gas No. 4.

6. Layer up the lentil mixture and fried aubergines in a shallow ovenproof dish, ending with aubergines.

7. Make the cheese sauce as per page 31 and pour it over the aubergines.

8. Bake for about 20 minutes until brown and bubbly.

CORN FRITTERS WITH FRESH TOMATO SAUCE
Serves 4

The tangy and juicy fresh tomato sauce perfectly offsets the richness of corn fritters making a nutritious supper dish.

Preparation time: 20 mins.   *Cooking time: 43 mins.*

Fresh tomato sauce (see page 55)
¼ pt (150ml) fritter batter (see page 23)
11 oz (312g) can sweetcorn, drained

1. Make the tomato sauce as per page 55.

2. Make the batter as per page 23.

3. Stir the drained sweetcorn into the batter and deep fry teaspoonfuls for 3-4 minutes. Drain on kitchen paper.

STUFFED AUBERGINES
Serves 4

This recipe was given to me by a friend who spends a lot of time in Spain. It makes a lovely summer supper when served with brown rice.

Preparation time: 40 mins.   *Cooking time: 55 mins.*

2 medium/large aubergines
Salt
¼ pt (150ml) oil
1 large onion, peeled and chopped
2 cloves garlic, peeled and chopped
14 oz (397g) can peeled tomatoes
Freshly ground black pepper
Grated Parmesan cheese

1. Halve the aubergines and scoop out the flesh with a spoon. Sprinkle the shells with salt and leave to drain for 30 minutes.

2. Cut the aubergine flesh into pieces, sprinkle with salt and leave to drain.

3. Rinse the shells and flesh and pat dry with kitchen paper.

4. Heat 3 tablespoons of the oil and gently fry the chopped aubergine, onion and garlic for 12 minutes.

5. Add the tomatoes and plenty of pepper and cook gently until the mixture has thickened (about 25 minutes).

6. Meanwhile, pre-heat oven to 180°C (350°F) or Gas No. 4.

7. Stand the aubergine shells in a shallow ovenproof dish and pour over the remainder of the oil, making sure the shells are well coated inside and out.

8. Fill the shells with the tomato mixture and sprinkle with Parmesan cheese.

9. Bake for 30 minutes, brushing the exposed edges of the shells with oil occasionally.

MEXICAN PANCAKES   *Serves 8-10*

Pancakes need moist fillings otherwise the overall dish will be too dry. This creamy tomato and mushroom stuffing, which is spiced 'hot' with chilli, is just the thing. Serve with boiled brown rice to give added texture.

Preparation time: 10 mins.   *Cooking time: 40 mins.*

½ pt (300ml) pancake batter (see page 22)
2 tablsp oil
1 onion, peeled and chopped
6 oz (175g) mushrooms, roughly chopped
12 oz (350g) tomatoes
1 tablsp tomato purée
2 oz (50g) packet cashew nuts (optional)
1 chilli, finely chopped
Salt and freshly ground black pepper
5 fl oz (142ml) carton soured cream

1. Make the pancake batter.

2. Heat the oil and gently fry the onion and mushrooms until tender, about 12 minutes.

3. Meanwhile, skin the tomatoes by spearing with a fork and dipping in boiling water for one minute. The skin then easily peels off. Roughly chop the flesh.

4. Stir the tomato flesh, tomato purée, nuts (if using), chilli, salt, pepper and soured cream into the mushroom mixture and cook gently for a further 8 minutes.

5. Make and cook the pancakes as per stages 3 and 4 opposite.

6. Divide the tomato mixture between the pancakes and roll up.

Tip: Unfilled pancakes can be cooked well in advance. They keep in the fridge for 2-3 days or they can be frozen by layering up the pancakes in between greaseproof paper and then wrapping the whole lot in foil. The pancakes will defrost in a very short time and can then be re-heated in a low oven.

SPINACH AND CREAM CHEESE PANCAKES

Serves 4

Serve with brown rice.

Preparation time: 15 mins.   *Cooking time: 40 mins.*

½ pt (300ml) white or wholemeal pancake batter
  (see page 22)
8 oz (225g) spinach
Little oil for frying
4 oz (110g) cream cheese
5 fl oz (150ml) carton soured cream
2 oz (50g) Cheddar cheese, grated

1. Make the pancake batter as per page 22. Leave to stand.

2. Wash and shred the spinach and cook in a little boiling
    water for 8 minutes until tender. Drain well.

3. Meanwhile, make the pancakes: Heat a teaspoon of oil in
    an 8″ (20cm) frying pan and pour in just enough batter to
    cover the base thinly.

4. Cook for 2-3 minutes, then turn and cook the other side.
    Continue cooking the other pancakes in the same way.
    (The mixture makes about 8 pancakes.)

5. Pre-heat oven to 180°C (350°F) or Gas No. 4.

6. Mix the spinach with the cream cheese and use the
    mixture to fill the pancakes.

7. Roll each pancake up and place in a shallow ovenproof
    dish.

8. Spoon over the soured cream and sprinkle with grated
    cheese.

9. Bake for about 10 minutes until the cheese has melted.

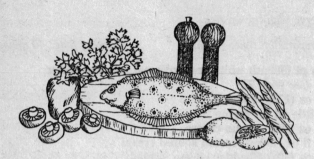

7. FISH

Surprisingly a 4 oz (110g) portion of fish provides half the daily amount of protein needed by the average person. It is also low in saturated fats but rich in vitamins and minerals. Fish is quick to cook and there is little or no waste. The bad news is that most varieties, due mainly to huge quantities being exported, are expensive which puts them outside the realms of this book.

Unlike most other fresh food, the price of fish is not so much governed by season but by quality and weather. My fishmonger tells me that the cost doubles at the mere mention of a gale warning! Price can fluctuate enormously even from day to day.

My best advice is to make friends with a specialist fishmonger who will be pleased to talk all day about his subject. He will advise on 'best buys', quality, suggest ways of cooking, and bone and prepare the fish in a more professional way than the average cook can ever hope for.

Fish is best eaten as soon as possible after it is caught. However, while there is nothing to compare with a piece of fresh fish, some frozen varieties are cheaper, and quite adequate for making fish cakes and pies. Cod, haddock, plaice and coley are to be found in most supermarkets, usually in 2 lb (900g) bags.

Below is a list of those fish which, generally speaking, are at the cheaper end of the market.

Mackerel: A rich oily fish, mackerel is delicious grilled or marinaded in sharp flavours like lime or chilli. Should be eaten really fresh; after a day or so the flesh deteriorates in texture and taste.

Smoked Mackerel: Needs no further cooking and the flavour is preferred by many to the fresh fish. It is excellent in salads and pâtés.

Herring: English herrings have a higher oil content and superior flavour but they deteriorate rapidly. *Baltic herrings* stay better-looking for a longer time but may not be as fresh as they seem. Herrings should be eaten very fresh so be careful where you buy. Herrings are usually grilled and, like mackerel, respond well to sharp piquant sauces. They are also good pickled or 'soused' and served cold with salad.

Ask your fishmonger to bone mackerel or herring. I find they are much nicer to eat and are usually more acceptable to children this way.

Sardines: These are imported frozen from the Mediterranean but are reasonably priced and are good grilled or barbecued.

Sardines canned in oil: These are well worth keeping in the store cupboard for cheap and tasty snacks.

Pilchards: These are mature sardines which are caught around the coast of Devon and Cornwall. They should be eaten very fresh and can be grilled or barbecued. My fishmonger suggests wrapping the pilchards in a lettuce leaf, which keeps the fish moist, and then discarding the lettuce after grilling.

Coley: Until fairly recently coley was deemed fit only for the cat, but now with the high cost of other white fish, coley is enjoying the popularity it deserves. It is good in pies or fish cakes or baked and served with a sauce.

Cod: A traditional favourite which is available in fillets or steaks. Coat in batter or breadcrumbs before frying, or grill and serve with parsley and lemon butter. Also good for pies and fish cakes.

Whiting: A delicate-, almost bland-, tasting fish but

nonetheless it is good for fish cakes, pies, pâtés and terrines.

Haddock: Similar to cod but with a slightly softer texture. Cook in the same way as cod.

Smoked Haddock: With the public awareness of the danger of artificial colourings there is a trend away from the bright yellow fillets towards those with a paler colour which are cured and preserved naturally. Usually poached in milk, it is excellent for adding flavour to kedgeree and fish cakes.

Plaice: Another traditional favourite, plaice can be grilled whole, filleted and fried, or stuffed, rolled and baked in milk. Fillets tend to be thin and need very little cooking time.

Tuna: By comparison with the fresh fish, canned tuna is cheap. It is a good store cupboard standby with its solid and meaty flesh being ideal for salads and pasta dishes.

FISH PUFFS
Serves 4

These make a nice light supper dish and are usually popular with children. Serve with salad and plenty of tartare (see page 79) or tomato sauce.

Preparation time: 20 mins.   *Cooking time: 10 mins.*

8 oz (225g) white fish (cod, haddock or coley)
4 tablsp milk
Salt and freshly ground black pepper
1 oz (25g) margarine
1 oz (25g) flour
1 size 3 egg, beaten
Oil for frying

1. Put the fish, milk, salt and pepper in a small saucepan, bring to boil and simmer for 5-10 minutes depending on thickness. Drain but reserve the liquid.

2. Melt the margarine in the saucepan, add the flour and stir for 1 minute over a low heat.

3. Gradually add the fish liquor (use 4 tablespoonfuls and make up with cold milk if necessary). Cook for a further

couple of minutes, stirring all the time, until the mixture forms a thick ball leaving the sides of the pan clean.

4. Remove from the heat and beat in the beaten egg a little at a time.

5. Flake the fish and mix it thoroughly into the egg mixture. Leave to cool.

6. Heat a deep pan of oil and drop in teaspoons of the mixture.

7. Fry for about 8 minutes until the fish balls are crisp and golden. Drain on kitchen paper.

Note: The food should bubble very gently; if the oil is too hot the mixture will be burnt on the outside and raw inside.

FISH CAKES   *Serves 4*

Fish cakes are a good way of making a little fish go a long way and also encouraging children to eat fish when otherwise they may not be keen. By making your own you know exactly what has gone into them!

Preparation time: 20 mins.   *Cooking time: 20 mins.*

1 lb (450g) potatoes, peeled and cut into pieces
8 oz (225g) white fish (cod, haddock or coley)
Salt and freshly ground black pepper
1 tablsp freshly chopped parsley (optional)
Little finely grated lemon rind (optional)
1 size 3 egg, beaten
Breadcrumbs)
Beaten egg   )   for coating

1. Cook the potatoes in boiling, salted water for about 15-20 minutes until tender. Drain and mash.

2. Meanwhile, put the fish in enough salted water to barely cover it and cook over a low heat for about 8-10 minutes depending on thickness. Then drain the fish, peel off the

skin and pull out any bones.

3. Flake the fish into a bowl and mix in the mashed potato, salt, pepper, parsley and lemon rind (if using) and the beaten egg. Bind well and allow to cool.

4. Turn the mixture on to a floured board and form into 8 patties.

5. Brush both sides with beaten egg and then dip into breadcrumbs.

6. Fry the fish cakes in oil (use enough to come half way up the cakes) for about 8-10 minutes on each side until crisp and golden. Drain on kitchen paper.

Tip: Instead of flavouring the fish cakes with lemon rind, use 2 teaspoons of Worcestershire sauce.

SMOKED MACKEREL PÂTÉ
Serves 4 as a main course or 6 as a starter

With a food processor the preparation of this tasty pâté takes literally seconds. However even by hand it only takes 10 minutes. Although not essential the cayenne pepper gives a 'bite' to the pâté without making it at all 'hot'. Serve with plenty of fresh brown bread for a perfect light lunch or supper.

Preparation time: 10 mins.   *Cooking time: none*

8 oz (225g) smoked mackerel (about 2 fillets)
4 oz (110g) carton cream cheese
Juice 1 lemon
½ level teasp cayenne pepper (optional)
Salt and freshly ground black pepper

1. Peel the skin off the mackerel, remove any bones and then mash the flesh in a bowl.

2. In a separate bowl soften the cheese with a wooden spoon and then gradually mix in the lemon juice alternately with the mackerel.

3. Stir in the cayenne, a little salt and plenty of black pepper. Mix well, press into a shallow dish and chill before serving.

CHIP SHOP FISH SUPPER   *Serves 4*

A firm family favourite when served with chips and peas. Use cod, haddock, coley or whiting.

Preparation time: 10 mins.   *Cooking time: 10 mins.*

¼ pt (150ml) fritter batter (see page 23)
2 tablsp flour
Salt and freshly ground black pepper
4 fillets white fish

1. Make the batter as per page 23.

2. Mix the flour, salt and pepper together and coat the fish with the seasoned flour.

3. Dip the fish in the batter and deep fry for about 10 minutes according to thickness. Drain on kitchen paper.

Tip: I always feel there is something missing if I eat fried fish without tartare sauce, but a small ready-made jar is ridiculously expensive. It's much cheaper to make your own! Stir a chopped pickled gherkin, a few chopped chives or parsley and a teaspoon of gherkin vinegar into some mayonnaise. Jars of pickled gherkins will keep for weeks.

GRILLED MACKEREL

Allow one small to medium sized fish per person. Mackerel is particularly good served cold and goes well with spicy or tangy flavours. Simply trickle the cooked fish with lemon or lime juice, plenty of freshly ground black pepper and serve with salad and crusty bread.

Preparation time: 5 mins.   *Cooking time: 10 mins.*

Grilled Mackerel continued

Small to medium sized mackerel, boned
Oil
Salt and freshly ground black pepper

1. Pre-heat grill to medium.

2. Make 3 or 4 cuts in the mackerel, season the inside of the fish with salt and pepper and brush the outside with oil.

3. Grill for about 5 minutes on each side. If liked the skin can be removed before serving.

   Herrings can be cooked in the same way.

BAKED MACKEREL WITH VEGETABLES

Serves 4

Mackerel fillets cooked on a bed of diced vegetables make a good light supper dish. Serve with plenty of fresh crusty bread.

Preparation time: 15 mins.   *Cooking time: 25-30 mins.*

2 tablspn oil
1 onion, peeled and chopped
1 red pepper, diced
4 oz (110g) button mushrooms, sliced
1 lb (450g) courgettes, diced
4 small mackerel OR 2 large, boned
Salt and freshly ground black pepper

1. Pre-heat the oven to 180°C (350°F) or Gas No. 4.

2. Heat the oil and gently fry the onion, pepper, mushrooms and courgettes for 5 minutes. Drain and place in a shallow ovenproof dish.

3. Flatten out the mackerel and, if large, cut into two lengthways.

4. Season with salt and pepper, place on top of the vegetables. Cover with foil and bake for 25-30 minutes.

8. MEAT

This chapter includes recipes for cooking cheaper cuts of meat which are often overlooked, but which when cooked properly can be just as tender and tasty as expensive cuts. Ideas are also given for cooking well known and popular 'cheapies' – sausages, sausagemeat, mince and canned meat like corned beef and spam.

By mixing with cheaper ingredients like lentils, beans and vegetables, meat can be 'stretched' to make economical pies and casseroles. Many joints at the bottom end of the price range are best boned and then stuffed and rolled, which not only makes the meat go further but adds flavour too. Some joints, like brisket and silverside which have been slowly pot-roasted, can be finished off in a hot oven to simulate the flavour and appearance of more expensive beef roasting joints.

Among some new ideas are traditional favourites just right for a cold winter's evening or, as one elderly relative used to say, 'as warm and comforting as a red flannel petticoat.'

The price of meat varies from shop to shop but I have yet to find an independent butcher who was not cheaper than a supermarket. The cost of weekly meat purchases can be substantially reduced with a little knowledge of the various cuts. It will pay to find a friendly and reliable butcher who will give advice on best buys and ways of cooking.

It is often argued that meals using cheaper cuts of meat are time-consuming to make. It's true that coarser meat takes longer to cook but in most cases preparation is quick and easy, which to my mind is the worst part of cooking. Take stews and casseroles for example; meat and vegetables can all be cooked together so no additional accompaniments have to be prepared. Once in the oven it is almost impossible to spoil such meals. On the other hand, a fried or grilled meal not only demands expensive meat but also the constant presence of the cook.

LAMB

New Zealand lamb is cheaper than English. I am told that only top quality meat is exported so it does seem to offer good value for money. Check comparisons yourself before buying.

Breast: A rather fatty cut but good boned, stuffed and rolled. Can be slow roasted, boiled, braised and casseroled. Bear in mind that the bones amount to about half the breast's weight but they can be used to make stock.

Middle Neck: Nice meaty chops which should be cooked slowly. Excellent for Lancashire Hot Pot and Irish Stew.

Scrag End: An unfortunate term; although the meat has a rather high proportion of fat and bone, it is cheap and makes excellent flavourful stews.

Shoulder: More expensive than the above-mentioned cuts but just about within the price range to be included in the book! Usually sold as whole or half shoulder on the bone. Can be roasted as it is, or boned, stuffed and rolled for more economy.

Liver and Kidney: Well flavoured and tender enough to be grilled or fried.

Minced Lamb: Now available from some supermarkets and butchers. Use for pies, rissoles, and classic dishes like Greek Moussaka.

BEEF

Brisket: Usually sold boned and rolled. A good flavour and excellent for pot-roasting with vegetables or can be served cold with salad.

Silverside: A boneless joint which is a bit more expensive than brisket, but leaner. For best results cook slowly, either by pot-roasting, braising or boiling. Ideal for finishing off in a hot oven to simulate the flavour and appearance of more expensive roast beef.

Leg and Shin: Usually sold as stewing beef. Should have long slow cooking; use in stews, casseroles and pies and for classic dishes like curry, goulash and steak and kidney pudding.

Chuck Steak: Usually sold as braising steak which means that it needs less cooking time than stewing cuts. Lean and tender, chuck can be used in the same ways as leg and shin, but also for dishes like Cornish Pasties (see page 95).

Flank: Usually sold as mince but can be used for stewing or making stock.

Oxtail: Once common on the menu of most households, this flavoursome meat needs long, slow cooking, but makes a rich, hearty stew or soup.

Minced Beef: Use for beefburgers, rissoles, pies, meat loaves and classics like Cottage Pie and Spaghetti Bolognese.

Liver and Kidney: Those from ox and bullock are the cheapest but strong in flavour and coarse in texture. Both need slow gentle cooking and should be casseroled and stewed rather than grilled or fried. However, calf's liver and kidney are tender and delicate in flavour and are considered the best and most expensive.

PORK

Unlike beef or lamb, even the cheaper cuts of pork are suitable for roasting.

Spare Rib: Usually sold in chops or steaks, spare rib can be roasted, braised in pineapple juice, casseroled in a sauce or used for the Chinese dish, sweet and sour pork in batter.

Blade: A roasting joint on the bone, or it can be boned, stuffed and rolled.

Shoulder: Sometimes known as 'hand' or 'spring', the joint can be roasted on the bone or the meat can be boned, stuffed and rolled or used for casseroles.

Belly: A rather fatty cut which is usually sold in strips and can be used in casseroles or risottos. Alternatively, the joint can be boned, stuffed and rolled and then roasted.

Ribs: American-style ribs are cut from the belly, leaving a little meat surrounding individual rib bones. Usually barbecued or roasted in a sweet and sour or Oriental type of sauce.

Minced Pork: Now available from some supermarkets and butchers; makes a change from beef for rissoles, burgers and pies.

Liver and Kidney: Pig's liver has a pronounced flavour and soft texture, but is excellent for making pâté. The kidneys are larger than lamb's and are good halved and then grilled or fried.

BACON

Obtained from a side of pork which has been salted over a period of time. Although more expensive, bacon is also smoked by exposure to smoke from slow burning hardwood. Streaky bacon, from the belly, is the cheapest and is ideal for adding flavour to omelettes, pies and risottos. Bags of bacon bits, sold by butchers, are usually the most economical way of buying bacon.

Bacon Joints: Hock, shoulder and collar are the most moderately priced with gammon the most expensive. After boiling, the joints can be served hot with parsley sauce, cold with salad or finished off in the oven to crisp and brown the fat. Left-over bits and pieces can be used for croquettes, soups and pies.

ROAST STUFFED SHOULDER OF LAMB
Serves 6-8

The average sized shoulder of lamb, when boned, stuffed and rolled, should serve between 6-8 people. It therefore makes two economical meals for an average family. Eat it hot the first night, with gravy, roast potatoes and greens, and cold the next with salad. This recipe uses home-made stuffing but similar packet mixes are available and are one of the few things as cheap to buy as make.

Preparation time: 15 mins.   *Cooking time: About 2 hours*

1 oz (25g) margarine
1 tablsp clear honey
2 oz (50g) dried apricots, snipped into pieces
2 oz (50g) sultanas
Small piece onion, peeled and finely chopped
4 oz (110g) fresh breadcrumbs
½ level teasp dried OR 1 teasp chopped fresh rosemary
1 size 2 egg, beaten
Salt and freshly ground black pepper
3½-4½ lb (1.6-2.2kg) shoulder of lamb, boned

1. Pre-heat oven to 170°C (325°F) or Gas No. 3.

2. Put the margarine and honey in a small saucepan and melt over a low heat.

3. Remove from the heat and stir in the apricots, sultanas, onion, breadcrumbs, rosemary, beaten egg, salt and pepper. Bind the mixture well together.

4. Lay the lamb flat on a board, fat side down, and spread on the stuffing to within 2″ (5cm) of the edge.

5. Roll up the meat and tie with string or secure with skewers to prevent it unrolling during cooking.

6. Weigh the joint and calculate cooking time at 40 minutes per 1 lb (450g).

7. Stand the joint in a roasting tin, brush with oil and sprinkle with salt. Cook for the required time.

Tip: When par-boiling potatoes for the accompanying roasties, cook twice as many than you need. Then on the following night you've got a supply of cold potatoes to make a heap of scrumptious Hash Browns (see page 27) to go with the cold lamb and salad.

POT-ROASTED STUFFED BREAST OF LAMB
Serves 4

Breast of lamb is cheap but rather thin and not particularly meaty. Stuffing with sausagemeat and then slowly roasting it with a selection of vegetables is a good way of cooking.

Preparation time: 10 mins.   *Cooking time: 2 hours*

1 breast of lamb, boned
12 oz (350g) sausagemeat
1 onion, peeled and chopped
2 carrots, sliced
½ small turnip, peeled and diced
1 stock cube
Little water

1. Pre-heat oven to 150°C (300°F) or Gas No. 2.

2. Lay the lamb flat on a board, fat side down, and spread on the sausagemeat to within 2″ (5cm) of the edge.

3. Roll up and tie loosely with string or secure with skewers to prevent the meat unrolling during cooking.

4. Put the onion, carrot and turnip in a deep lidded roasting tin or casserole dish.

5. Crumble in the stock cube and add enough water to just cover the vegetables. Mix well.

6. Stand the meat on top of the vegetables, put on the lid and cook for about 2 hours until the meat is tender.

   If preferred, the gravy can be thickened by mixing a little flour and water to a paste, and then gradually stirring it into the hot liquid a few minutes before the meat is ready.

LAMB AND LENTIL CASSEROLE   *Serves 4-6*

An all-in-one meal which is lovely served with plenty of fresh crusty bread.

Preparation time: 10 mins.   *Cooking time: 2-2½ hours*

1 tablsp oil
2 lb (900g) middle neck lamb chops
6 oz (175g) red lentils
1 onion, peeled and chopped
8 oz (225g) carrots, sliced
2-3 sticks celery (depending on size)
14 oz (397g) can peeled tomatoes
Salt and freshly ground black pepper
1 pt (570ml) stock OR water

1. Pre-heat oven to 170°C (325°F) or Gas No. 3.

2. Heat the oil and brown the chops quickly on both sides.

3. Put the chops and all remaining ingredients into a large lidded casserole.

4. Cook for 2-2½ hours until the meat is tender.

LANCASHIRE HOT POT   *Serves 4-6*

Simple, tasty, filling and cheap. Serve with green vegetables in season.

Preparation time: 15 mins.   *Cooking time: 2 hours*

2 lb (900g) potatoes, peeled and sliced
2 onions, peeled and sliced
2 lb (900g) middle neck lamb chops
Salt and freshly ground black pepper
3 lambs' kidneys, skinned and sliced (optional)
½ pt (300ml) stock OR 1 stock cube and
   ½ pt (300ml) water
Little oil or melted margarine

1. Pre-heat oven to 170°C (325°F) or Gas No. 3.

2. Put a layer of potatoes and all the onions in the bottom of a large lidded casserole dish.

3. Cut excess fat off the chops and lay them on top of the potato. Season with salt and pepper.

4. Add the sliced kidneys if using and then pour on the stock.

5. Top with remaining sliced potatoes, uniformly arranged to give an attractive finish.

6. Brush the top of the potato with oil or melted margarine, put on the lid and cook for about 2 hours until the meat and potatoes are tender. If the casserole becomes too dry add a little water.

7. About 20 minutes before the end of the cooking time, remove the lid and turn the oven up to 200°C (400°F) or Gas No. 6 to allow the potatoes to brown.

BRAISED BRISKET OF BEEF

Makes 2 meals for 4 people

A 2½-3 lb (1.1-1.4kg) piece of brisket should serve four people to eat hot one day and then the remainder made into rissoles for supper the next. Use about 2 lb (900g) of vegetables (unprepared weight) which can include potatoes, onions, turnips, parsnips, carrots, mushrooms, celery, leeks or fennel. A can of baked beans also makes a tasty addition.

Preparation time: 15 mins.   *Cooking time: 2½ hours*

1 tablsp oil
2½-3 lb (1.1-1.4kg) piece boned and rolled brisket
8 oz (225g) potatoes, peeled and cut into pieces
8 oz (225g) carrots, sliced
1 large onion, peeled and cut into pieces
8 oz (225g) parsnips, peeled and quartered
2 sticks celery, cut into pieces
4 oz (100g) mushrooms, left whole unless large
Salt and freshly ground black pepper
½ pt (300ml) water
2 rounded teasp flour

1. Pre-heat oven to 150°C (300°F) or Gas No. 2.

2. Heat the oil in a frying pan and brown the meat all round and on both ends, about 5 minutes.

3. Put all the prepared vegetables in a large lidded casserole dish, season with salt and pepper and pour in the water.

4. Lay the meat on the vegetables, cover and cook for 2½ hours.

5. About 15 minutes before the end of the cooking time thicken the gravy by mixing the flour to a paste with a little cold water and then adding it to the hot liquid in the casserole. Leave the lid off to crisp the meat.

Tip: If the meat and vegetables are too bulky to allow the lid to fit on the casserole dish properly, cover the top with foil, folding it tightly down over the edge.

RISSOLES   *Serves 4*

Any cold cooked meat can be used to make rissoles. This

recipe is designed to use left-over beef from the previous recipe. For a tasty hearty meal serve with Hash Browns (see page 27) and baked beans or, for a lighter supper, potato salad and greens.

Preparation time: 20 mins.   *Cooking time: 30 mins.*

1 lb (450g) potatoes, peeled and cut into pieces
8 oz (225g) cold cooked beef
1 onion, peeled and grated
1 tablsp Worcestershire sauce
Salt and freshly ground black pepper
1 size 2 egg, beaten

1. Cook the potatoes in boiling, salted water until tender, about 12-15 minutes. Drain and then mash.

2. Meanwhile, mince or finely chop the meat.

3. Mix the mashed potato, meat, onion, Worcestershire sauce, salt, pepper and egg and bind well.

4. Divide mixture into 4, roll each in flour and press into patties about ½" (1cm) thick.

5. Shallow fry for 10-15 minutes on each side.

BEEF STEW WITH DUMPLINGS   *Serves 4*

Any root vegetable is suitable for this rich brown stew including turnips, parsnips, potatoes, leeks, carrots and fennel. Aim for about 1-1½ lb (450g-700g) total weight.

Preparation time: 15 mins.   *Cooking time: 2½-3 hours*

2 tablsp oil
1 large onion, peeled and sliced
1 green pepper, sliced
6 oz (175g) mushrooms, halved if large
3 sticks celery, cut into pieces

1-1½ lb (450-700g) stewing beef, cubed
2 tablsp flour
Salt and freshly ground black pepper
1 teasp yeast extract OR 1 beef stock cube
½ pt (300ml) water
Dumplings (see page 18)

1. Pre-heat oven to 150°C (300°F) or Gas No. 2.

2. Heat the oil and fry the onion, pepper, mushrooms and celery for 5 minutes until softened. Lift out with a slotted spoon and place in a large lidded ovenproof casserole dish.

3. Coat the meat in flour, salt and pepper and fry in the same pan for about 5 minutes until browned. (Add a touch more oil if necessary.)

4. Turn the meat into the casserole dish and stir in any excess flour, the yeast extract or crumbled stock cube and water.

5. Cook with a lid on for 2½-3 hours until the meat is tender.

6. Meanwhile, make the dumplings as per page 18 and pop them into the casserole about 20 minutes before the end of the cooking time.

Tip: By using braising steak, although a little more expensive, the cooking time can be reduced (1½-2 hours).

MEAT, POTATO AND ONION PIE   *Serves 4*

This is an economical pie which is just as good served with hot vegetables as salad.

Preparation time: 15 mins.   Cooking time: 2 hours 20 mins.

8 oz (225g) stewing beef, cut into small pieces
2 onions, peeled and chopped
12 oz (350g) potatoes, peeled and diced

continued overleaf

Meat, Potato and Onion Pie continued
1 beef stock cube
1 tablsp flour
½ pt (300ml) water
Salt and freshly ground black pepper
8 oz (225g) short crust pastry (see page 20)

1. Pre-heat oven to 150°C (300°F) or Gas No. 2.

2. Put the meat, onions, potato, crumbled stock cube, flour, water, salt and pepper into a lidded casserole dish and mix well.

3. Cook for about 2 hours until the meat is tender. Stir occasionally during cooking and if the mixture becomes too dry add a spot more water. Remove casserole from oven and allow to cool slightly.

4. Meanwhile, make the pastry as per page 20.

5. Turn oven up to 200°C (400°F) or Gas No. 6.

6. Roll out half the pastry and use to line an 8″ (20.5cm) pie plate or shallow pie dish.

7. Spoon the meat mixture into the pastry case and dampen the edges.

8. Roll out remaining pastry and use to cover the meat.

9. Trim the edges, then pinch together with thumb and forefinger.

10. Make a cross in the top of the pastry with a sharp knife, then brush with milk.

11. Bake for about 20 minutes until the pastry is golden brown.

CUMBERLAND PIE   *Serves 4*

This is a variation of Cottage Pie with a crunchy topping of breadcrumbs and cheese. Serve with green vegetables in season.

Preparation time: 10 mins.   *Cooking time: 30 mins.*

8 oz (225g) carrots, sliced thinly
2 tablsp oil
1 large onion, peeled and roughly chopped
1 lb (450g) minced beef
Salt and freshly ground black pepper
1 beef stock cube
14 oz (397g) can peeled tomatoes
2 lb (900g) potatoes, peeled and cut into pieces
Knob margarine or butter
Little milk
2 oz (50g) tasty Cheddar cheese, grated
2 oz (50g) fresh white breadcrumbs

1. Cook the carrots in boiling, salted water until just tender, about 8 minutes.

2. Meanwhile, heat the oil in a frying pan and sauté the onion for a few minutes until softened.

3. Add the mince, salt and pepper, roughly breaking the meat up with a fork. Cook for about 8 minutes until browned.

4. Crumble in the stock cube and add the tomatoes and drained carrots. Mix well and cook gently for a couple of minutes.

5. Turn the mixture into an ovenproof dish and allow to cool.

6. Meanwhile, cook the potatoes in boiling, salted water for about 15 minutes until tender. Drain.

7. Mash the potatoes with the margarine or butter and a little milk to a softish consistency.

8. Pre-heat oven to 180°C (350°F) or Gas No. 4.

9. Spoon the potato on to the meat mixture, flatten down with a fork, and then top with mixed grated cheese and breadcrumbs.

10. Bake for about 20 minutes until the topping is brown and crisp.

STUFFED MARROW   *Serves 4*

Marrows are really cheap in the autumn so make the most of them with this tasty stuffing.

Preparation time: 10 mins.   *Cooking time: 1 hour*

1 marrow
1 lb (450g) lean minced beef
1 onion, peeled and chopped
3 oz (75g) packet herb stuffing mix
Salt and freshly ground black pepper
1 size 3 egg, beaten
Oil for brushing

1. Peel the marrow with a sharp knife, then cut in half horizontally and scoop out the seeds.

2. Pre-heat oven to 180°C (350°F) or Gas No. 4.

3. Mix the meat, onion, stuffing mix, salt, pepper and beaten egg together and press the mixture into the hollows in the two marrow halves.

4. Brush the marrow with oil, wrap in foil and bake for 1 hour.

CORNED BEEF HASH   *Serves 4*

It's hard to believe that ready-prepared versions of this basic meal are on the market, neatly surrounded by a glossy photograph! This tasty combination of corned beef, tomatoes and onion is topped with fluffy potato, and a family size serving costs a few pence more than one meagre convenience portion! It's quick to do too. Serve with vegetables or salad.

Preparation time: 15 mins.   *Cooking time: 35 mins.*

2 lb (900g) potatoes, peeled and cut into pieces
½ tablsp oil
1 large onion, peeled and chopped
12 oz (350g) can corned beef
14 oz (397g) can peeled tomatoes
Salt and freshly ground black pepper
4 tablsp milk
1 size 3 egg, beaten

1. Cook the potatoes in boiling, salted water for about 10 minutes until tender. Drain.

2. Heat the oil and sauté the onion for a few minutes until transparent. Lift out with a slotted spoon and put in a bowl.

3. Add the corned beef, tomatoes (with their juice), salt and pepper to the onion and mix well. Turn the mixture into an ovenproof dish.

4. Pre-heat oven to 200°C (400°F) or Gas No. 6.

5. Mash the potatoes, then beat in the milk and beaten egg to make a soft fluffy consistency.

6. Spoon the potato on top of the corned beef mixture and level off with a fork.

7. Cook for about 25 minutes until the potato is brown and crispy.

CORNISH PASTIES   *Makes 4*

A tasty mixture of meat, potatoes and onion, these pasties are good served hot or cold with vegetables or salad.

Preparation time: 30 mins.   *Cooking time: 1 hour*

8 oz (225g) short crust pastry (see page 20)
8 oz (225g) potatoes, diced
1 onion, peeled and chopped
8 oz (225g) chuck or braising steak, cut into small pieces
1 beef stock cube
Salt and freshly ground black pepper
1 tablsp water
Milk to glaze pastry

1. Pre-heat oven to 200°C (400°F) or Gas No. 6.

2. Make the pastry as per page 20.

3. Mix the potatoes, onion, meat, crumbled stock cube, salt, pepper and water together.

4. Roll out the pastry and then using a saucer or plate about 6″ (15cm) in diameter, cut out 4 rounds. (You will probably have to roll out the scraps to get the fourth round.)

5. Divide the meat mixture between the pastry rounds, brush the edges with milk and then fold over, crimping the edges firmly between thumb and forefinger.

6. Place the pasties on a greased baking tray and brush the tops with milk.

7. Bake for 12 minutes then turn the oven down to 170°C (325°F) or Gas No. 3 and cook for a further 45-50 minutes.

VIENNESE STEAK   *Serves 4*

Braising (long slow cooking in the oven) is a nice way of cooking coarser cuts of steak. Beer or lager (use the cheapest you can find) creates a rich flavourful gravy but cut costs further by substituting water for the beer and using a crumbled stock cube instead of brown sugar.

Preparation time: 15 mins.   *Cooking time: 2 hours*

3 tablsp oil
1 large onion, peeled and sliced
4 oz (110g) button mushrooms
2 level tablsp flour
Salt and freshly ground black pepper
1¼ lb (575g) braising steak
1 level tablsp soft brown or demerara sugar
½ pt (300ml) beer or lager

1. Pre-heat oven to 150°C (300°F) or Gas No. 2.

2. Heat the oil and gently fry the onion and mushrooms for 10 minutes.

3. Mix the flour and a generous amount of salt and pepper together and coat the steak with the mixture.

4. Lift out the onion and mushrooms with a slotted spoon and place them in a large, not too deep, ovenproof dish.

5. Using the same frying pan, brown the meat for a couple of minutes on each side and then place on top of the vegetables.

6. Stir the sugar, beer or lager and any remaining seasoned flour into the pan, heat until it bubbles and then pour over the meat.

7. Cover tightly with foil or put on a lid and cook for about 2 hours until the meat is tender.

OXTAIL STEW WITH DUMPLINGS   *Serves 4*

Serve this traditional meal on a cold winter's night accompanied by lightly cooked shredded cabbage. Ask your butcher to cut the oxtail into pieces.

Preparation time: 15 mins.   Cooking time: 2 hours 50 mins.

1 oxtail, jointed
2 onions, peeled and cut into pieces
2 carrots, sliced
2 tablsp oil
2 beef stock cubes
2 level tablsp flour
¾ pt (425ml) water
Salt and freshly ground black pepper

1.   Pre-heat oven to 150°C (300°F) or Gas No. 2.

2.   Fry the oxtail, onions and carrots in the oil for about 20
     minutes until the meat and onions are lightly browned.

3.   Using a slotted spoon, lift the meat and vegetables into a
     large lidded casserole dish.

4.   Stir the crumbled stock cubes and flour into the pan juices
     and gradually add the water, stirring all the time.

5.   Bring to the boil, pour into the casserole and season with
     salt and pepper.

6.   Cook for 2½-3 hours until the meat is tender.

7.   Make the dumplings as per page 18 and pop into the
     casserole 20 minutes before the end of the cooking time.

ROAST STUFFED BELLY OF PORK   Serves 4-6

Personal preference will dictate whether or not you remove the
skin from the pork. I usually do, leaving a thin layer of fat
which crisps nicely during cooking. The stuffing is a quick
version which alleviates the chore of making breadcrumbs.
Serve with roast potatoes, green vegetables in season and gravy
(see page 32).

Preparation time: 10 mins.   *Cooking time: 2 hours*

2 slices bread, cut into small cubes
1 tablsp freshly chopped parsley) OR 2 level teasp
1 tablsp freshly chopped sage   ) mixed dried herbs
Salt and freshly ground black pepper
1 small onion, peeled and finely chopped
1 size 3 egg, beaten
2-3 tablsp boiling water
2-2½ lb (900g-1.1kg) piece belly of pork, boned

1. Pre-heat oven to 170°C (325°F) or Gas No. 3.

2. Put the bread, herbs, salt, pepper and onion into a small
    bowl and bind together with beaten egg and water. Leave
    to cool for a few minutes.

3. Cut the skin off the pork, if liked, and place skin side
    down on a board.

4. Spread the stuffing down the centre of the meat, roll up
    loosely and either tie with string or secure with a skewer
    to prevent the meat unrolling during cooking.

5. Sprinkle the rolled joint with salt and roast for about 2
    hours.

PORK AND APPLE PIE   *Serves 4*

The traditional combination of pork and apple makes a tasty
pie. Serve with potatoes and vegetables in season.

Preparation time: 15 mins.   *Cooking time: 40 mins.*

1 tablsp oil
1 onion, peeled and chopped
1 lb (450g) minced pork
8 oz (225g) cooking apples, peeled, cored and sliced
1 oz (25g) flour
1 tablsp dry mustard

continued overleaf

Pork and Apple Pie continued

Salt and freshly ground black pepper
½ pt (300ml) water
8 oz (225g) short crust white or wholemeal pastry
  (see page 20)

1. Heat the oil and fry the onion for 5 minutes.

2. Add the meat and brown quickly for a further 5 minutes.

3. Stir in the apples, flour, mustard, salt, pepper and water.

4. Bring to the boil and then simmer for 10 minutes, stirring occasionally.

5. Pour the mixture into a pie dish and allow to cool.

6. Meanwhile, make the pastry as per page 20.

7. Pre-heat oven to 190°C (375°F) or Gas No. 5.

8. Roll out the pastry slightly larger than the top of the pie dish.

9. Cut off a ½" (1cm) strip from round the edge of the pastry and put this strip round the damped rim of the dish.

10. Damp the strip with water and use remaining pastry to cover the pie. Trim off excess pastry and pinch edges between thumb and forefinger.

11. Make a cross in the centre of the pie to let out steam and brush the pastry with milk.

12. Bake for about 20 minutes until the pastry has nicely browned.

BOILED BACON JOINT

A 3 lb 8 oz-3 lb 12 oz (1.6-1.7kg) bacon joint should be enough for four people to eat sliced with roast potatoes, green vegetables and Parsley Sauce (see page 31) the first night and then the remainder used to make Ham and Egg Croquettes (see page 106) or Breakfast-Style Omelette (see page 44) and Pea and Ham Soup (see page 41). Hock, shoulder and collar joints are cheaper than gammon. Unsmoked is also cheaper than smoked. Supermarkets sometimes offer special discounts but check prices with your butcher too.

Preparation time: 10 mins.   Cooking time: 1 hour 45 mins.

**3 lb 8 oz-3 lb 12 oz (1.6-1.7kg) shoulder of bacon
Demerara sugar**

1. Put the bacon into a large saucepan of cold water. Bring slowly to the boil and then discard the water. (This gets rid of excess salt.)

2. Calculate the cooking time at 25 minutes per pound (450g) and then put the bacon in a saucepan of fresh cold water.

3. Bring to the boil and then simmer for the allotted time.

4. Towards the end of the cooking time pre-heat oven to 220°C (425°F) or Gas No. 7.

5. Lift out the bacon and cut off the skin leaving about ½″ (1.25cm) of fat intact.

6. Score the fat into diamonds and sprinkle liberally with demerara sugar.

7. Bake in the oven for about 15 minutes until the topping is brown and crispy. Then slice and serve as above.

Tip: Don't throw away the bacon stock. Use to make Pea and Ham Soup (see page 41). Leave the stock to go cold overnight when the fat will have formed a solid layer and can easily be spooned off and discarded.

BACON AND ONION DUMPLING   *Serves 4*

Traditionally this meal would probably be accompanied by swede and mashed potato but I particularly like it with Bombay Potatoes (see page 27) and a basic salad.

Preparation time: 15 mins.   *Cooking time: 2 hours*

8 oz (225g) streaky bacon or bacon bits, chopped
1 large onion, peeled and chopped
8 oz (225g) self-raising flour
1 level teasp salt
4 oz (110g) shredded suet
1 size 3 egg, beaten
¼ pt (150ml) milk

1.   Fry the chopped bacon and onion for 10 minutes. Drain.

2.   Meanwhile, mix the flour, salt and suet in a bowl, then stir in the bacon and onion.

3.   Make a well in the centre, pour in the egg and milk, mixing to a soft dropping consistency. Add a little more milk if necessary.

4.   Grease a 1½ pt (900ml) pudding basin and spoon in the suet mixture.

5.   Cover tightly with foil and stand the basin in a large saucepan. Pour in enough water to come halfway up the basin.

6.   Bring to simmering point, then put the lid on the saucepan and cook slowly for 2 hours. Remember to top up the water should the level drop due to evaporation.

POTATO AND BACON BAKE   *Serves 4*

It's not often you'll see cream in a book on economical cooking! But this recipe is cheap enough to be able to indulge a little luxury.

Preparation time: 15 mins.   *Cooking time: 1 hour*

8 oz (225g) lean bacon bits, diced
Few drops oil
2 lb (900g) potatoes, peeled and sliced thinly
1 large onion, peeled and sliced thinly
Salt and freshly ground black pepper
5 fl oz (142ml) carton single cream
3 tablsp milk
2 oz (50g) tasty Cheddar cheese, grated

1. Fry the bacon in the oil for 15 minutes.

2. Meanwhile, cook the potatoes and onion in boiling, salted
    water for 5 minutes. Drain.

3. Pre-heat oven to 180°C (350°F) or Gas No. 4.

4. Layer up the potatoes and onions with the bacon in a deep
    ovenproof dish, sprinkling with salt and pepper in between
    the layers.

5. Pour on the cream and milk and top with grated cheese.

6. Bake for 45 minutes until the top is brown and crispy.

LEEK AND HAM PIE   *Serves 4*

Don't buy the best cans of ham for this recipe as you're only
chopping it up! The ham formed from selected cuts of pork is
much cheaper and just as good.

Preparation time: 20 mins.   *Cooking time: 40 mins.*

1 lb (450g) leeks, sliced
1 oz (25g) margarine
1 oz (25g) flour

continued overleaf

Leek and Ham Pie continued

3 fl oz (100ml) milk + 3 fl oz (100ml) leek water
3 oz (75g) Cheddar cheese, grated
Salt and freshly ground black pepper
7 oz (200g) can ham, diced
8 oz (225g) short crust pastry (see page 20)

1. Cook the leeks in boiling, salted water until just tender, about 5-8 minutes. Drain but reserve the water.

2. Meanwhile, melt the margarine in a small saucepan, add the flour and cook over a low heat for 1 minute.

3. Gradually stir in the liquid (half milk and half leek water).

4. Bring to the boil, stirring all the time, and cook for a couple of minutes until the sauce has thickened.

5. Stir in the grated cheese and adjust seasoning if necessary.

6. Mix the leeks and ham into the sauce and allow to cool.

7. Pre-heat oven to 200°C (400°F) or Gas No. 6.

8. Meanwhile, make the pastry as per page 20.

9. Roll out half the pastry and use to line an 8″ (20.5cm) shallow pie dish.

10. Spoon in the ham and leek mixture.

11. Brush the edges of the pastry with milk or water.

12. Roll out remaining pastry and cover the pie, pressing the edges together and pinching between thumb and forefinger.

13. Brush the top with milk and bake for about 30 minutes until golden brown.

PANCAKES STUFFED WITH HAM AND MUSHROOMS
Makes 8-10

Ham and mushrooms in a tasty cheese sauce is a well loved combination. Try this filling with wholemeal pancakes (see page 22).

Preparation time: 10 mins.   *Cooking time: 50 mins.*

½ pt (300ml) wholemeal pancake batter
2 oz (50g) margarine
6 oz (175g) mushrooms, roughly chopped
1 oz (25g) flour
½ pt (300ml) milk
3 oz (75g) tasty Cheddar cheese, grated
Salt and freshly ground black pepper
4 oz (110g) cooked ham, diced

1. First make the pancake batter.

2. Then melt the margarine in a small saucepan and gently fry the mushrooms until tender, about 10 minutes. Remove with a slotted spoon into a bowl.

3. Stir the flour into the pan juices and cook for 1 minute. Gradually add the milk and then bring to the boil, stirring until the sauce thickens.

4. Add the grated cheese and stir over a low heat until it has melted. Season to taste with salt and pepper.

5. Pre-heat oven to 180°C (350°F) or Gas No. 4.

6. Add the ham to the mushrooms and mix in a little of the cheese sauce.

7. Make and cook the pancakes as per stages 3 and 4 on page 73.

8. Divide the mixture between the pancakes, roll up and place them in a shallow ovenproof dish.

9. Pour over the remaining cheese sauce and bake for about 20 minutes until golden and bubbling.

HAM AND EGG CROQUETTES   *Makes 8*

This is a good recipe to use the last oddments of meat after boiling a bacon joint (see page 100). Cooked ham could also be used. Serve with jacket potatoes and baked beans.

Preparation time: 30 mins.   *Cooking time: 5 mins.*

1½ oz (35g) margarine
1½ oz (35g) flour
¼ pt (150ml) milk
6 oz (175g) cooked ham or bacon, finely chopped
3 eggs, hard boiled and chopped
Salt and freshly ground black pepper
1 tablsp freshly chopped parsley (optional)
Beaten egg   )
Breadcrumbs) for coating

1. Put the margarine, flour and milk in a small saucepan and stir over a low heat until thickened.

2. Add the ham or bacon, eggs, salt, pepper and parsley if using and mix well. Allow to go cold.

3. Turn the mixture on to a floured surface, divide into 8 and roll each into a croquette shape.

4. Coat with beaten egg and then breadcrumbs.

5. Deep fry for about 5 minutes until crisp and golden brown. Drain on kitchen paper.

PARSON'S PIE   *Serves 4*

Breaking up the sausagemeat and adding tomatoes renders the filling soft and moist in texture. The pie is equally good served hot with vegetables or cold with salad.

Preparation time: 25 mins.   *Cooking time: 45 mins.*

1 large onion, peeled and chopped
1 tablsp oil
12 oz (350g) sausagemeat
14 oz (397g) can peeled tomatoes, drained
Salt and freshly ground black pepper
8 oz (225g) short crust pastry (see page 20)

1. Fry the onion in the oil for about 10 minutes until lightly brown. Drain.

2. Meanwhile, put the sausagemeat into a bowl and break it up with a fork, then mix in the tomatoes, seasoning and onion.

3. Pre-heat oven to 200°C (400°F) or Gas No. 6.

4. Make the pastry as per page 20.

5. Roll out half the pastry and use to line an 8″ (20.5cm) shallow pie dish. Brush the edges with milk or water.

6. Spoon in the sausage mixture.

7. Roll out remaining pastry and cover the filling, pressing the edges well together. Trim off excess pastry and then pinch the edge together between thumb and forefinger.

8. Brush the top of the pie with milk and bake for 15 minutes. Turn oven down to 180°C (350°F) or Gas No. 4 and cook for a further 30 minutes.

Tip: Don't throw the tomato juice away. Use it up in soups or casseroles.

MEAT LOAF (1)   *Serves 4*

This is as good served hot with vegetables as served cold with
salad.

Preparation time: 5 mins.   *Cooking time: 1½ hours*

1 lb (450g) sausagemeat
1 large onion, peeled and finely chopped
1 cooking or eating apple, peeled, cored and grated
3 oz (85g) packet sage and onion stuffing mix
Salt and freshly ground black pepper
1 size 2 egg, beaten

1. Pre-heat oven to 200°C (400°F) or Gas No. 6.

2. Mix all the ingredients together using your hands to bind
    well.

3. Pack the mixture into a greased loaf tin or shape into a loaf
    and wrap in foil.

4. Bake for about 1½ hours.

MEAT LOAF (2)   *Serves 4*

The addition of oats not only adds fibre but an interesting and
succulent texture to the meat loaf. Serve hot with mashed or
hash brown potatoes or cold with potato salad and greens.

Preparation time: 10 mins.   *Cooking time: 1 hour 20 mins.*

1 lb (450g) minced beef
4 oz (110g) streaky bacon, chopped
1 onion, peeled and chopped
4 oz (110g) rolled oats or porridge oats
Salt and freshly ground black pepper
1 tablsp Worcestershire sauce
1 size 2 egg, beaten
2 tablsp freshly chopped parsley (optional)

1. Pre-heat oven to 170°C (325°F) or Gas No. 3.

2. Mix all the ingredients together using your hands to bind the mixture well.

3. Form the mixture into a thick sausage shape and wrap in greased foil. Bake for about 1 hour 20 minutes.

SPAM FRITTERS   *Serves 4*

A cheap standby of years gone by. Luncheon meat or corned beef can be treated in the same way. Serve with creamed potatoes and a good mixed salad to counteract the richness.

Preparation time: 10 mins.   *Cooking time: 6 mins.*

12 oz (350g) can spam
¼ pt (150ml) fritter batter (see page 23)
Oil for deep frying

1. Cut the spam into thickish slices.

2. Make the batter as per page 23.

3. Dip the spam slices into the batter and fry in hot oil for about 6 minutes until golden brown. Drain on kitchen paper.

Tip: If using corned beef, chill the tin overnight in the fridge. The corned beef will be much easier to handle if it is hard before coating with batter.

LIVER WITH MUSHROOMS   *Serves 4*

In this recipe liver, mushrooms and onion are cooked in mushroom soup which makes a tasty and easy sauce. Serve with noodles, rice or potatoes.

Preparation time: 5 mins.   *Cooking time: 45 mins.*

1 lb (450g) liver (any variety will do)
1 level tablsp flour
Salt and freshly ground black pepper
2 tablsp oil
1 large onion, peeled and sliced
4 oz (110g) mushrooms, sliced if large
15 oz (425g) can mushroom soup

1. Pre-heat oven to 180°C (350°F) or Gas No. 4.

2. Cut the liver into pieces and coat with seasoned flour.

3. Heat the oil and brown the liver on both sides. Remove with a slotted spoon and place into an ovenproof casserole dish.

4. Fry the onion and mushrooms in the same pan for about 5 minutes, then stir in any excess flour (from coating the liver) and the soup.

5. Pour the mixture over the liver and cook for 45 minutes.

LIVER AND BACON PROVENÇAL   *Serves 4*

The traditional combination of liver and crispy bacon in a rich tomato sauce. Serve with potatoes or boiled rice.

Preparation time: 10 mins.   *Cooking time: 1 hour*

1 lb (450g) liver (any variety will do)
2 oz (50g) flour
2 tablsp oil
8 rashers streaky bacon, each cut in 3 pieces
1 large onion, peeled and chopped
14 oz (397g) can peeled tomatoes
1 tablsp Worcestershire sauce
Salt and freshly ground black pepper
1 beef stock cube
¾ pt (425ml) water

1. Slice the liver into thick strips and coat with the flour.

2. Heat the oil and brown the liver quickly on both sides. Lift out with a slotted spoon and place in an ovenproof casserole.

3. Fry the bacon and onion in the same pan, adding more oil if necessary, for about 15 minutes until golden.

4. Meanwhile pre-heat oven to 180°C (350°F) or Gas No. 4.

5. Stir in any excess flour (from coating the liver), tomatoes, Worcestershire sauce, salt, pepper, crumbled stock cube and water.

6. Bring to the boil and then pour the mixture over the liver.

7. Put a lid on the casserole, or cover with foil, and cook for 45 minutes.

STEAK AND KIDNEY PUDDING   *Serves 4*

A real traditional dish which is cheap and easy to make and filling and delicious to eat.

Preparation time: 20 mins.   *Cooking time: 4 hours*

8 oz (225g) suet pastry (see page 21)
1 tablsp oil
1 large onion, peeled and chopped
12 oz (350g) stewing beef, cut into pieces
4 oz (110g) lamb's kidneys, cut into pieces
2 level tablsp flour
Salt and freshly ground black pepper
3 tablsp water

1. Grease a 1½ pt (900ml) pudding basin.

2. Make the suet pastry as per page 21.

3. Roll out three-quarters of the pastry and use to line the basin.

4. Heat the oil and fry the onion for a couple of minutes.

5. Toss the beef and kidney in the flour and add some salt and pepper.

6. Add the meat mixture to the onion and fry for about 6-8 minutes until the meat is browned.

7. Stir in the water and mix well.

8. Pour the meat mixture into the pudding basin.

9. Bring a large saucepan of water to the boil.

10. Roll out the remaining pastry to form a lid the size of the top of the basin.

11. Damp the pastry lining and press on the lid, sealing the edges well.

12. Cover the top tightly with foil.

13. Put the basin in the saucepan of water and simmer very gently for about 4 hours. (As the water evaporates top up the saucepan.)

14. Turn the cooked pudding out on to a serving dish.

9. CHICKEN AND TURKEY

Pound for pound chicken and turkey offer consistently good value for money. Both butchers and supermarkets sell poultry so compare prices before buying.

The cost of chicken varies according to the cut and whether the bird is free-range, fresh or frozen. Whole chickens, quarters, legs, breasts and thighs are available either with the bone or ready-boned, the latter cuts being more expensive.

Not all butchers have such a wide choice but some sell boneless breast joints (the prime cut) and these are often cheaper than supermarket equivalents.

For everyday family cooking, whole chickens or frozen joints are probably the most economical.

Almost the same choice of turkey cuts is now available, including boneless joints, cubes, mince and strips suitable for stir-fries.

CHICKEN CASSEROLE   *Serves 4*

The beauty of casseroles is their versatility. Just about any combination of ingredients can be used. Substitute the vegetables in this recipe for whatever needs using up. The bacon adds a nice flavour but is by no means essential.

Preparation time: 10 mins.   Cooking time: 1 hour 20 mins.

2 tablsp oil
2 rashers streaky bacon, chopped
4 chicken joints
1 large onion, peeled and chopped
2 sticks celery, sliced
4 oz (110g) button mushrooms
1 oz (25g) flour
¾ pt (425ml) stock or stock cube and water
Salt and freshly ground black pepper

1. Heat the oil and fry the bacon and chicken joints until lightly brown, about 15 minutes.

2. Meanwhile, put the onion, celery and mushrooms into a large lidded casserole dish.

3. Pre-heat oven to 180°C (350°F) or Gas No. 4.

4. Lift out the chicken joints and put them into the casserole.

5. Stir the flour into the pan with the bacon and cook for 1 minute.

6. Gradually add the stock, stirring all the time. Bring to the boil and simmer for a couple of minutes until the mixture thickens. Season to taste with salt and pepper.

7. Pour the liquid into the casserole and cook for about 1 hour until the chicken is tender.

CHICKEN AND MUSHROOM BAKE   *Serves 4*

Chicken and mushrooms in a savoury sauce with a crisp potato topping. Serve with fresh crusty bread and salad.

Preparation time: 30 mins.   Cooking time: 1 hour 15 mins.

2 chicken quarters
1 large onion, peeled and cut into pieces
8 oz (225g) mushrooms, sliced
Salt and freshly ground black pepper
1½ lb (700g) potatoes, peeled and sliced thinly
1 oz (25g) flour
1 oz (25g) margarine
¼ pt (150ml) milk
¼ pt (150ml) stock from cooked chicken
Oil for brushing potato

1. Put the chicken, onion, mushrooms, salt and pepper into a saucepan and pour in enough water to come halfway up the chicken.

2. Bring to the boil and then simmer gently for about 45 minutes until the chicken is tender.

3. Meanwhile, cook the potatoes in boiling, salted water for 5 minutes. Drain.

4. Pre-heat oven to 200°C (400°F) or Gas No. 6.

5. Lift out the chicken, remove the flesh from the bones and cut into small pieces.

6. Drain the mushrooms and onion, reserving ¼ pt (150ml) of the stock.

7. Put the flour, margarine, milk and stock into a saucepan and whisk over a low heat until thickened.

8. Stir the chicken, mushrooms and onion into the sauce and adjust seasoning if necessary.

9. Turn the mixture into a shallow ovenproof dish, top with the sliced potato and brush with oil.

10. Bake for about 30 minutes until the potatoes are brown and crispy.

CHICKEN CURRY   *Serves 4*

Serve with white or brown rice.

Preparation time: 15 mins.   *Cooking time: 1 hour*

2 tablsp oil
4 chicken pieces
1 onion, peeled and chopped
1 green pepper, cut into chunks
1 red pepper, cut into chunks
2 medium sized potatoes, peeled and cut into chunks
1 level tablsp curry powder or more to taste
1 stock cube
14 oz (397g) can peeled tomatoes
½ pt (300ml) water

1. Heat the oil and brown the chicken on all sides. Remove to a lidded ovenproof casserole dish.

2. Fry the onion, peppers and potatoes for about 10 minutes, adding more oil if necessary. Lift out with a slotted spoon and add to the casserole.

3. Pre-heat oven to 180°C (350°F) or Gas No. 4.

4. Stir the curry powder and crumbled stock cube into the pan juices, then add the tomatoes and water.

5. Bring to the boil and then pour into the casserole dish.

6. Cook for about 1 hour until the chicken is tender.

TURKEY AND VEGETABLE STIR-FRY   *Serves 4*

Use turkey or chicken for this quick and tasty meal. Cooked meat from a bacon joint makes a good alternative. The vegetables in this recipe are only a guide, just about any can be used. Aim for about 2 lb (900g) total weight and cook only until the vegetables are barely tender. Overcooked vegetables are just not allowed! Serve with brown rice.

Preparation time: 15 mins.   *Cooking time: 28 mins.*

4 tablsp oil
8 oz (225g) turkey OR chicken, cut in strips
1 red pepper, sliced
4 oz (110g) mushrooms, sliced
4 oz (110g) courgettes, sliced
3 spring onions, cut into pieces
3 sticks celery, sliced
8 oz (225g) broccoli, broken into small florets
8 oz (225g) carrots, cut into matchsticks
2 tablsp soy sauce

1. Heat 2 tablespoons of the oil and fry the turkey or chicken for about 8 minutes until sealed on all sides.

2. Add the remaining oil and all the prepared vegetables and fry over a medium heat for about 15 minutes, stirring frequently.

3. Add the soy sauce and continue stir-frying for a further 5 minutes.

10. DESSERTS

Perhaps born of a chilly climate and the hardship of two wars, the U.K.'s repertoire of warming, filling and economical puddings leaves the rest of the world standing. Steamed and baked sponges awash with jam or syrup, hearty apple dumplings, suet roly-poly, fritters and pancakes, many have remained classics and, although perhaps buried in the subconscious, are sadly not in regular use. It's a tradition worth reviving if only once a week. Hot puddings are cost-effective and satisfying for a hungry family.

Since cream plays a large part in most cold desserts, and cream is expensive, few chilled desserts have been included in the book — except in Chapter 12, Entertaining on a Budget, when you are permitted to indulge a small luxury!

Fruit should be washed thoroughly under cold running water before eating or preparing for cooking. In the case of soft fruit — raspberries, strawberries and blackberries — keep washing to a minimum to save damaging the fruit. For best results, put the fruit in a colander and rinse gently under the cold tap. Drain well.

Fresh fruit always makes a good dessert and the following

list gives a rough guide to seasons when prices reach their lowest. Make the most of the refreshing taste of raw fruit as it is packed with vitamins and needs little or no preparation or embellishment.

Apples: All year round with home-grown eaters and cookers reaching a glut in the autumn.

Apples, Crab: September-October. Excellent for jelly and other preserves.

Apricots: December-February and May-August. Apricots should be just ripe; over-ripe and the flesh is soft and woolly. Use for jam, puddings or raw in fruit salad.

Bananas: All year round. Use in fruit salad, fritters, cakes and tea-breads.

Blackberries: Pick 'free' in the hedgerows in autumn. Excellent for jelly, jam, puddings, pies and crumbles.

Blackcurrants: July. Use for jam, pies and crumbles.

Cherries: June-August for eating raw in fruit salad; July-August for cooking cherries. Use for jam, pies and puddings.

Elderberries: Pick 'free' in the hedgerows or waste ground in late summer or early autumn. Good for home-made wine or mixed in equal quantities with apples to make jelly.

Gooseberries: June. Make excellent jam or use in pies, crumbles or purée and mix with custard and cream for the classic Gooseberry Fool.

Grapefruits: All year round. Good as a refreshing starter to a rich main course or mixed with orange segments for Florida Cocktail.

Grapes: All year round, but reach lowest price from April-August. Use in fruit salad or tarts.

Greengages: July-September. Use for jam, puddings and pies.

Loganberries: July-August. Delicious eaten raw in fruit salad or use for gâteaux and meringue-based desserts.

Melons: At their cheapest in June and July. There are several varieties of melon, including Water, Canteloup, Charentais and Honeydew. Excellent eaten raw as a starter, dessert or in fruit salad. Also good for jam, chutney and pickle.

Nectarines: July-August (home-grown). December-May and

August-September (imported). Similar to a peach but with a smooth shiny skin. Excellent raw or in fruit salad.

Oranges: All year round.

Peaches: June-August (home-grown). January-March and June-September (imported). Eat raw or in fruit salad or in desserts such as Peach Melba.

Pears: September-March. Eat raw in fruit salad or in classic dishes like Pears in Red Wine or Pears Belle Hélène (page 139) where pear halves are served with ice cream and chocolate sauce.

Pineapples: June-July. Eat raw sliced and sprinkled with icing sugar or as part of a fruit salad.

Plums: July-September (home-grown). January-April and May-July (imported). Excellent for jam, pies and crumbles.

Raspberries: July-August. Delicious eaten raw on their own, in fruit salad or in gâteaux and meringue-based desserts.

Redcurrants: July. Use for pies, puddings, jelly and cold desserts such as Redcurrant Compote.

Rhubarb: December-March (early or forced). March-June (outdoor). Early rhubarb is pale pink with a delicate fresh flavour. Delicious cooked for a few minutes in a little water and sugar and then served with custard or cream. Outdoor rhubarb is thicker with a more acidic flavour. Use the stalks in pies, crumbles, puddings or for chutney or jam. Don't eat the leaves.

Strawberries: June-July. Delicious on their own with cream or in fruit salad or use for gâteaux and meringue-based desserts.

Tangerines, Clementines, Satsumas and Mandarins: October-February. Small citrus fruits, all resembling a small orange. Eat raw or in fruit salad or can be used for mixed citrus fruit marmalade.

Dried Fruit: In the winter months when fresh fruit is expensive, dried fruit offers an economical and nutritious alternative. Prunes, figs, apples, peaches, apricots and pears are available which are rich in fibre, protein, vitamins and minerals. Some no-soak varieties are now on the market, although other varieties will require soaking in cold water overnight before cooking.

Most dried fruit is sprayed with preservative which gives a pleasing moist appearance. Wash the fruit in hot water before cooking. Likewise sulphur dioxide is used to preserve colour; remove this by cooking the fruit in boiling water for one minute and then discard the water.

BREAD AND BUTTER PUDDING   *Serves 4-6*

Don't feed your stale bread to the ducks, your need is probably greater than theirs!

Preparation time: 10 mins.   *Cooking time: 1 hour*

4 slices stale bread
1 oz (25g) butter or margarine
2 oz (50g) sultanas
2 tablsp brown or white sugar
2 size 2 eggs
¾ pt (425ml) milk

1. Spread the bread with butter or margarine and cut each slice diagonally into four.

2. Grease a shallow ovenproof dish and lay in half the bread and butter pieces, butter side up.

3. Sprinkle on the sultanas and sugar, then top with remaining pieces of bread.

4. Beat the eggs, pour on the milk and then strain the liquid on to the pudding.

5. If possible leave to stand for 1 hour, or at least 30 minutes.

6. Meanwhile, pre-heat oven to 170°C (325°F) or Gas No. 3.

7. Lay a thick layer of newspaper in the base of a large roasting tin and stand the bread and butter pudding on top. Pour enough water into the roasting tin to come halfway up the pudding dish.

8. Bake for about an hour by which time the custard should have nicely set with a brown and puffy top.

Tip: In my experience most people, especially children, prefer the crispy parts of bread and butter pudding. By using a larger shallow dish, rather than a smaller deeper one, there is more surface area to go crispy.

STEAMED SYRUP SPONGE   *Serves 6*

Serve this popular perennial with custard.

Preparation time: 10 mins.   *Cooking time: 1½ hours*

4 oz (110g) soft margarine
4 oz (110g) caster sugar
2 size 2 eggs, beaten
6 oz (175g) self-raising flour
½ tablsp milk
3 tablsp golden syrup

1. Cream the margarine and sugar together until light and fluffy.

2. Beat in the eggs a little at a time.

3. Using a metal spoon fold in the sieved flour and milk to give a soft dropping consistency.

4. Grease a 1½ pt (900ml) pudding basin and spoon the syrup into the bottom.

5. Top with the sponge mixture.

6. Cover the basin tightly with foil and stand it in a large saucepan.

7. Pour in enough water to come halfway up the basin, put on the lid and simmer over a low heat for 1½ hours. Remember to top up the water should the level drop through evaporation.

Variations:

Jam Sponge: Put 2-3 tablespoons of jam in the bottom of the basin.

Spotted Dick: Fold 2 tablespoons of sultanas into the sponge mixture.

Fruit Sponge: Put some stewed or tinned fruit in the bottom of the basin.

Cherry Sponge: Halve some glacé cherries, then toss them in flour before adding to the sponge mixture.

PINEAPPLE UPSIDE-DOWN CAKE   *Serves 4*

Golden syrup and pineapple combine to make a delicious gooey base to a standard sponge mixture.

Preparation time: 10 mins.   *Cooking time: 25 mins.*

4 tablsp golden syrup
8 oz (225g) pineapple rings
4 oz (110g) margarine
4 oz (110g) caster sugar
2 size 2 eggs, beaten
4 oz (110g) self-raising flour

1. Pre-heat oven to 180°C (350°F) or Gas No. 4.

2. Grease and flour an 8″ (20.5cm) sandwich tin.

3. Put the syrup and 1 tablespoon of the pineapple juice in the base of the sandwich tin and lay the pineapple rings on top.

4. Cream the margarine and sugar together until light and fluffy.

5. Gradually add the eggs beating well between each addition.

6. Fold the sieved flour into the mixture and spoon on top of the pineapple.

7. Bake for about 20-25 minutes until the sponge is lightly

brown and firm to the touch. Turn the cake out of the tin upside-down, and serve.

SYRUP TART
Serves 4

An old favourite which children usually can't get enough of.

Preparation time: 15 mins.   *Cooking time: 20 mins.*

8 oz (225g) short crust pastry (see page 20)
6 tablsp golden syrup
2 oz (50g) fresh white breadcrumbs

1. Pre-heat oven to 200°C (400°F) or Gas No. 6.

2. Make the pastry as per page 20 and use it to line a 7-8″ (18-20.5cm) flan ring or sandwich tin.

3. Spoon the syrup into the pastry case and sprinkle the breadcrumbs on top.

4. Bake for about 20 minutes.

BLACKBERRY JELLY
Serves 4-6

This is a particularly nice way of serving blackberries and encourages children to eat fresh fruit.

Preparation time: 10 mins.   *Cooking time: none*

1 tablet raspberry or blackcurrant jelly
8 oz (225g) blackberries

1. Make up the jelly according to manufacturer's instructions.

2. Chill until quite cold and then stir in the blackberries and leave until completely set.

Tip: Other economical desserts can be made with virtually any fruit in season. Try diced apple and pear in lemon jelly or orange segments in orange jelly.

11. BUDGET CAKES

When it comes to quality there is nothing quite like a home-made cake. A couple of slices are a good wholesome fill-me-up for hungry children when they come home from school. Cake also makes a good standby for an after-supper dessert.

Although cake-making is a fascinating art, it is not difficult. All are made with a few simple ingredients and if you have flour, margarine, sugar, eggs and some dried fruit in stock, you can always make a cake!

The following examples are designed to be easy on your pocket and easy on your time too.

To test if a cake is cooked, run a thin skewer into the centre. If it comes out clean the cake is cooked but, if any uncooked mixture is adhering to the skewer, leave the cake in the oven for a little longer. If the outside is looking too dark, turn the oven down a fraction.

DATE AND WALNUT LOAF

Nothing could be simpler to make than this delicious cake. No arm-aching mixing, whisking or beating either!

Preparation time: 8 mins.   *Cooking time: 50 mins.*

6 oz (175g) chopped dates
3 oz (75g) walnut pieces
4 oz (110g) demerara sugar
2 oz (50g) margarine
¼ pt (150ml) boiling water
1 size 2 egg, beaten
8 oz (225g) self-raising flour

1. Pre-heat oven to 180°C (350°F) or Gas No. 4.

2. Grease and flour a medium sized loaf tin.

3. Put the dates, nuts, sugar and margarine in a bowl and mix in the boiling water. Stir until the margarine has melted.

4. Stir in the beaten egg and then fold in the sieved flour.

5. Pour mixture into the loaf tin and bake for 45-50 minutes.

VAL'S TEA BREAD

Measure ingredients in a standard size cup throughout for perfect results. Use whatever dried fruit is in the cupboard — sultanas, seedless raisins or currants or a mixture of all three.

Preparation time: 5 mins. + overnight soaking
                                        Cooking time: 1 hour

1 lb (450g) dried fruit
1 cup black tea
1 cup demerara sugar
1 size 2 egg, beaten
1 cup self-raising flour

1. Soak the dried fruit, tea and sugar in a bowl overnight.

2. Pre-heat oven to 150°C (300°F) or Gas No. 2.

3. Grease and flour a medium size loaf tin.

4. Stir the egg into the fruit mixture and then fold in the sieved flour.

5. Pour into the tin and bake for about 1 hour.

BRAN AND APRICOT LOAF

Use the same standard size teacup throughout. The loaf is delicious sliced and buttered. If preferred sultanas can be used instead of apricots.

Preparation time: 5 mins. + 1 hour soaking time
Cooking time: 40 mins.

1 cup bran
1 cup soft brown sugar
4 oz (110g) dried apricots, snipped into small pieces
1 tablsp golden syrup
1 cup milk, warmed
1 cup self-raising flour

1. Put the bran, sugar, apricots, syrup and warm milk into a bowl, mix well and leave to stand for 1 hour.

2. Pre-heat oven to 180°C (350°F) or Gas No. 4.

3. Grease and flour a small or medium sized loaf tin.

4. Fold the sieved flour into the bran mixture, put into the tin and bake for about 40 minutes. Turn out and cool on a wire rack.

GENOESE SPONGE

This is a super-light sponge mixture which forms the basis of fruit gâteaux. It is ideal for a special occasion dessert or a tea-time treat when filled with jam and cream.

Preparation time: 20 mins.   *Cooking time: 15 mins.*

3 oz (75g) margarine
3 size 2 eggs
4 oz (110g) caster sugar
3 oz (75g) self-raising flour

1. Pre-heat oven to 180°C (350°F) or Gas No. 4.

2. Melt the margarine in a small saucepan or in a microwave.

3. Put the eggs and sugar in a large bowl and stand it over a saucepan of hot water.

4. Whisk the eggs and sugar until the mixture is light in colour and thick enough to retain the impression of the whisk, about 20 minutes.

5. Grease and flour two 7" (18cm) sandwich tins.

6. Fold the sieved flour and melted margarine, a little at a time into the whisked mixture until they are all used up. (The mixture must be very lightly mixed or volume will be lost, resulting in a flat, heavy cake.)

7. Pour the mixture into the prepared tins and bake for about 15 minutes until golden brown and springy to the touch.

8. Turn out on to a wire rack to cool.

Tip: For a special occasion dessert, split each sponge into two and then layer back together with fruit and whipped cream. Fresh raspberries or strawberries are particularly delicious. Dust the top with sieved icing sugar. A more economical version can be made using chopped canned peaches.

FLAPJACKS   *Makes about 16*

An easily made and nutritious chewy treat.

Preparation time: 10 mins.   *Cooking time: 20 mins.*

4 oz (110g) margarine
4 oz (110g) demerara OR soft brown sugar
3 tablsp golden syrup
8 oz (225g) porridge oats

1. Melt the margarine, sugar and syrup in a saucepan.

2. Meanwhile, heat oven to 180°C (350°F) or Gas No. 4.

3. Grease an 8″ (20.5cm) square tin.

4. Stir the oats into the syrup mixture and mix well.

5. Turn into the greased tin, press down and bake for about 20 minutes.

6. Mark into squares when hot and remove from tin when cold.

12. ENTERTAINING ON A BUDGET

Having guests to a meal can be a nightmare if you're short of cash. Luckily for most households informal entertaining has largely replaced the more formal dinner party.

Invariably it's the hostess who presents a simple, but attractive and tasty meal who is remembered more favourably than the one who has opened exotically packaged foil cartons from a chain store and spent a fortune in the process. Psychologically a little panache goes a long way. And that's what you have to do when entertaining on a shoestring — make a few expensive ingredients stretch or make humble ingredients appear more exciting.

The standard rule in menu planning is balance. Aim for a variety of ingredients and if you serve a substantial main course, precede or follow it with something light.

Finally, bear in mind that when you want to create an impression, the presentation of food and a cheerful welcome are more important than what you spend. The following menus are designed to cost about the same as take-away beefburgers and fries for 6 people.

SUGGESTED MENUS

Four three-course meals, one for each season, are suggested as well as two for more informal get-togethers. The recipes are designed to give a balance of flavours and each serves 6 people.

It's no time to experiment with guests due in an hour so try the ideas out beforehand to make sure you're happy with procedures, flavours and quantities.

Spring Menu
Smoked Mackerel Pâté
  (page 78)
Pork Chasseur
  New potatoes
  Peas and carrots
Caramel Custard

Summer Menu
Cheese Beignettes
Salmon Mousse
  Melba Toast
  Wild rice/mixed salad
Strawberry/
  Raspberry Gâteau

Autumn Menu
Egg Mayonnaise with
  Prawns
Carbonnade of Beef
  Brown or white rice
  Baked tomatoes
Pears Belle Hélène

Winter Menu
Florida Cocktail
Steak and Mushroom Pie
  Roast potatoes and
    parsnips
  Leeks in white sauce
Profiteroles

Informal Menus
Jambalaya
  Garlic bread
Lemon Crunch Pie

Lasagne
  Garlic bread
  Mixed salad
  Lemon Sorbet

SPRING MENU

PORK CHASSEUR   *Serves 6*

Supermarket freezer cabinets usually include packs of frozen pork steaks which are economical and ideal for this recipe. Serve with new potatoes, peas and carrots.

Preparation time: 10 mins.   *Cooking time: 40 mins.*

6 pork steaks
Oil
Salt and freshly ground black pepper
Knob margarine
1 large onion, peeled and chopped
6 oz (175g) mushrooms, sliced thinly
1 stock cube
14 oz (397g) can peeled tomatoes
5 fl oz (150ml) carton double cream

1. Pre-heat oven to 180°C (350°F) or Gas No. 4.

2. Put the pork steaks in a roasting tin, brush with oil and sprinkle with salt and pepper. Roast for about 40 minutes until the pork is tender. (If using frozen meat, make sure it is thoroughly defrosted before cooking.)

3. Meanwhile, heat 1 tablespoon of oil and the margarine in a frying pan and gently cook the onion and mushrooms for 8-10 minutes until tender.

4. Crumble in the stock cube.

5. Strain the tomatoes, roughly chopping them in the colander, but reserve the juice.

6. Stir the tomato flesh into the frying pan.

7. Now add the cream, a little salt and pepper and cook gently for a few minutes. If the sauce is too thick add a little of the tomato juice.

8. Transfer the pork to a serving dish and spoon over the sauce. If liked, sprinkle some chopped parsley on top.

CARAMEL CUSTARD   *Serves 6*

This popular dessert looks more attractive if cooked in individual stoneware cups or tin moulds. Alternatively, cook the custard in an ovenproof dish but it is more difficult to turn out and doesn't look so professional. For best results chill the cooked custards for several hours, or overnight, before serving.

Caramel custard is particularly nice served with a little fresh fruit and/or Continental-style biscuits.

Preparation time: 20 mins.   *Cooking time: 45 mins.*

For the caramel
5 oz (150g) caster sugar
7 fl oz (200ml) water

For the custard
1 pt (570ml) milk
1 oz (25g) caster sugar
4 size 2 eggs, beaten

1. Heat the water gently and dissolve the sugar slowly in it without boiling.

2. When thoroughly dissolved boil until the mixture caramelises, i.e. turns light brown and syrupy.

3. Pre-heat oven to 150°C (300°F) or Gas No. 2.

4. Put a thick layer of newspaper in the base of a roasting tin and half fill with water.

5. Stand 6 individual cups in the roasting tin and put in the oven to warm.

6. Bring the milk and sugar to boiling point, then pour over the beaten eggs and stir well.

7. Pour a little caramel into each warmed cup and twist it around to coat the bottom and part of the sides.

8. Strain the custard on to the caramel and cook for about 45 minutes. (One large dish will take about one hour.)

9. Remove the cups from the roasting tin and chill the custards in the fridge, preferably overnight. Loosen round the edge of the cups with a round-bladed knife and turn out into individual glass dishes.

SUMMER MENU

CHEESE BEIGNETTES   *Serves 6*

These light cheese puffs make a tasty and economical starter.
Serve 3 to 4 on a little shredded lettuce and add a garnish of
sliced tomato and cucumber.

Preparation time: 20 mins.   *Cooking time: 5 mins.*

1½ oz (40g) margarine
¼ pt (150ml) water
2 oz (50g) plain flour
2 size 3 eggs, beaten
2 oz (50g) tasty Cheddar cheese, grated
Salt and freshly ground black pepper
Grated Parmesan cheese for garnish (optional)
Cayenne pepper for garnish (optional)

1.   Melt the margarine in the water and bring to the boil.

2.   Remove from heat, add the sieved flour all at once and
     then beat until the mixture is smooth and leaves the sides
     of the pan clean.

3.   Beat in the eggs little by little.

4.   Stir in the grated cheese, salt and pepper.

5.   Heat a deep pan of oil and fry teaspoons of the mixture for
     about 5 minutes until golden brown and puffy. Drain on
     kitchen paper.

6.   Sprinkle with grated Parmesan cheese and a little cayenne
     pepper before serving if liked. Serve within 10 minutes of
     cooking.

Tip: The beignettes should sizzle gently when cooking; if the
oil is too cool they will be greasy and if it is too hot they will
be burnt on the outside and uncooked inside. For best results
use fresh oil.

SALMON MOUSSE

Serves 6

Even with the lower prices in recent years of farmed fish, fresh
salmon is still expensive. This light and creamy mousse is the
next best thing for warm summer evenings. It can be served in
any attractive dish but for a professional look use a tin mould.
I use a plain ring with a hole in the middle which always turns
out well.

Serve the mousse with melba toast (very thin slices of bread
toasted until crisp). Commercially made versions are available.
Wild rice and a good selection of salad vegetables complete the
perfect accompaniments.

Preparation time: 35 mins.
  plus several hours chilling   *Cooking time: none*

14.75 oz (418g) can red salmon
Approx. ¼ pt (150ml) milk
1 oz (25g) margarine
1½ oz (40g) flour
2 size 2 eggs, separated
1 teasp Worcestershire sauce
Juice ½ lemon
Salt and freshly ground black pepper
¼ level teasp cayenne pepper (optional)
2 teasp freshly chopped dill (optional)
5 fl oz (150ml) carton double cream, lightly whipped
4 level teasp powdered gelatine
3 tablsp hot water

1. Drain the salmon and make up the liquor to ½ pt (300ml)
   with milk.

2. Remove any skin from the fish and flake the flesh into a
   bowl.

3. Put the margarine, flour, salmon liquor and milk into a
   small saucepan and whisk over a low heat until thickened.

4. Remove from heat and stir in the egg yolks.

5. Stir the sauce into the salmon and leave to cool for a few minutes.

6. Stir in the Worcestershire sauce, lemon juice, salt, pepper, cayenne and dill if using and the lightly whipped cream.

7. Have ready a mould rinsed out with cold water but do not dry.

8. Sprinkle the gelatine on to the hot water and stir until dissolved. Set aside.

9. Whisk the egg whites until stiff.

10. Stir the dissolved gelatine into the salmon mixture and then fold in the egg whites thoroughly.

11. Pour the mixture into the wetted mould and chill in the fridge for several hours or overnight.

12. To turn out dip the mould in hot water for a few seconds. Invert a wet serving plate over the top of the mould, turn over and give the mould a good hard shake to release the mousse.

13. Garnish around the edge of the mousse with thin slices of lemon and cucumber. The central hole can be filled with sprigs of watercress and/or dill.

STRAWBERRY OR RASPBERRY GÂTEAU

Serves 6

This simple and delicious dessert can be made the day before serving and is an excellent choice for a summer dinner party.

Preparation time: 40 mins.   *Cooking time: 15 mins.*

Genoese Sponge (see page 128)
1 lb (450g) strawberries OR raspberries
10 fl oz (300ml) whipping OR double cream,
   lightly whipped
Caster sugar

1. Make the sponge as per page 128.

2. Meanwhile, slice the strawberries, reserving a few whole ones for the top, and sprinkle with sugar. If using raspberries leave whole and sprinkle with sugar.

3. When the sponge is cold, slice each horizontally and then layer back together with whipped cream, sliced strawberries or raspberries and a little of the juice.

4. Spread a layer of whipped cream over the top and decorate with whole strawberries or raspberries.

AUTUMN MENU

EGG MAYONNAISE WITH PRAWNS   *Serves 6*

Preparation time: 10 mins.   *Cooking time: 10 mins.*

6 size 3 or 4 eggs
Cress, sliced tomato and cucumber
6 tablsp mayonnaise
4 oz (110g) peeled prawns
Paprika pepper (optional)

1. Hard boil the eggs for 10 minutes. Hold under cold running water to prevent discolouration.

2. Meanwhile, arrange a little cress and a slice or two of tomato and cucumber on six small plates.

3. Shell and cut the eggs in two and place cut side down on the cress.

4. Spoon a little mayonnaise over the eggs and top with prawns.

5. Sprinkle with paprika if liked.

CARBONNADE OF BEEF   *Serves 6*

Beef cooked in beer is a classic tasty casserole. It is almost impossible to spoil so is ideal if unreliable guests are expected!

Preparation time: 10 mins.   *Cooking time: 2 hours*

2 lb (900g) chuck steak, cubed
1 large onion, peeled and roughly chopped
2 cloves garlic, peeled and finely chopped
2 tablsp oil
2 tablsp flour
2 teasp mustard powder
2 teasp soft brown sugar
2 teasp vinegar
Salt and freshly ground black pepper
1 level teasp mixed dried herbs OR 1 tablsp chopped
   fresh herbs
1 beef stock cube
½ pt (300ml) water
½ pt (300ml) beer or brown ale

1. Fry the meat, onion and garlic in the oil for about 10 minutes.

2. Meanwhile, pre-heat oven to 150°C (300°F) or Gas No. 2.

3. Stir the flour, mustard powder, brown sugar, vinegar, salt, pepper, herbs and crumbled stock cube into the meat and onion.

4. Transfer the mixture to a lidded ovenproof casserole and stir in the water and beer or brown ale. Mix well.

5. Cook for about 2 hours until the meat is tender, stirring occasionally.

Tip: The carbonnade can be served with plain boiled or pilau rice and green vegetables. However for the authentic French way, use a bread and mustard topping. Simply cut out 6 rounds from thin slices of bread, spread them with French mustard and pop the rounds on top of the carbonnade 15 minutes before serving. Return to the oven without a lid to crisp the bread.

PEARS BELLE HÉLÈNE *Serves 6*

This is a classic dessert of pears and ice cream topped with chocolate sauce. Use ripe plump pears and good quality ice cream.

Preparation time: 20 mins. *Cooking time: none*

4 oz (110g) plain chocolate
1 oz (25g) butter or margarine
2 tablsp milk
3 juicy pears
6 scoops vanilla ice cream

1. Put the chocolate and butter or margarine in a bowl and stand it in a saucepan of hot water to melt.

2. When well blended stir in the milk.

3. Meanwhile, cut each pear in half and remove the skin and core.

4. Put a scoop of ice cream in 6 individual glass bowls, top with a pear half and pour over a little chocolate sauce.

WINTER MENU

FLORIDA COCKTAIL *Serves 6*

This makes a light refreshing starter to the two hearty courses which follow.

Preparation time: 20 mins. *Cooking time: none*

3 grapefruit
3 oranges
6 glacé OR marachino cherries (optional)
Caster sugar

1. Segment the grapefruit and oranges as follows: Using a
    small sharp knife, remove the skin and pith by following
    the contour of the fruit. The flesh should be exposed.
    Holding the fruit in one hand over a basin, remove the
    segments by cutting down each side of the membrane.
    Finally squeeze the pulp to extract the juice.

2. Arrange the fruit attractively in six shallow glass bowls
    and top with a cherry.

3. Sprinkle a little caster sugar over the top.

STEAK AND MUSHROOM PIE   *Serves 6*

Few people can resist a home-made pie with tender chunks of
meat and mushroom, cooked in a dark rich gravy and topped
with a thick crust.

Preparation time: 15 mins.   *Cooking time: 2 hours.*

1½ lb (700g) chuck steak, cubed
1 large onion, peeled and roughly chopped
2 tablsp oil
8 oz (225g) large mushrooms, cut into pieces
1 tablsp flour
1 beef stock cube
Salt and freshly ground black pepper
½ pt (300ml) water
8 oz (225g) short crust pastry (see page 20)

1. Pre-heat oven to 150°C (300°F) or Gas No. 2.

2. Fry the meat and onion in the oil for about 5 minutes.

3. Stir in the mushrooms and cook for a further 5 minutes.

4. Turn the meat and vegetables into a lidded casserole and
    stir in the flour, crumbled stock cube, salt, pepper and
    water.

5. Cook for about 1½ hours until the meat is tender, stirring
    occasionally.

6. Meanwhile make the pastry as per page 20.

7. Turn the cooked meat mixture into an ovenproof pie dish and allow to cool slightly.

8. Meanwhile, turn the oven up to 200°C (400°F) or Gas No. 6.

9. Roll out the pastry slightly larger than the top of the pie dish. Next, cut off a strip from around the edge of the pastry, dampen the edge of the pie dish, and put the strip on it.

10. Dampen the strip and then use the remaining pastry to cover the pie. Trim off excess pastry and pinch the edges between thumb and forefinger.

11. Make a cross in the top of the pie with a sharp knife, cutting right through the pastry to allow the steam to escape, then brush the pastry with beaten egg or milk.

12. Bake for 20 minutes until nicely browned.

PROFITEROLES   *Makes 18-20*

Compared to buying ready-made these are cheap to make, if not a bit fiddly, but delicious!

Preparation time: 40 mins.   *Cooking time: 15-20 mins.*

1 oz (25g) margarine
¼ pt (150ml) water
2½ oz (75g) plain flour, sieved
2 size 4 eggs, beaten
5 fl oz (150ml) carton whipping OR double cream
2 oz (50g) plain chocolate
6 oz (175g) icing sugar

1. Pre-heat oven to 200°C (400°F) or Gas No. 6.

2. Melt the margarine in the water and bring to the boil.

3. Remove from heat, add the flour all at once and beat until the mixture forms a ball and leaves the side of the pan clean.

4. Gradually beat in the beaten eggs, beating well between each addition. (An electric beater makes the job less tiring.)

5. Put teaspoons of the mixture on to a wetted baking tray, spacing well apart, and bake for 15 to 20 minutes until crisp and golden brown. Cool on a wire rack.

6. Whip the cream until it just holds its shape.

7. Make a small hole in the bottom of each profiterole and spoon in a little cream. (The job is made much easier with a piping bag; if you don't have one see 'tip' below for making paper version.)

8. Now make the chocolate topping: Put the chocolate in a cup and stand it in a pan of hot water to melt. Do not overheat. Stir in a tablespoon of hot water and mix well.

9. Sieve the icing sugar into a bowl and stir in the chocolate. Add a little cold water if necessary to make a thick coating consistency.

10. Pile the profiteroles in a glass bowl and trickle over the chocolate topping.

Tip: To make a paper icing bag: Fold a 10″ (25cm) square of greaseproof or non-stick paper diagonally into a triangle. Holding the right angle of the triangle towards you, roll over one of the corners to meet it. Roll the second corner over in the opposite direction to meet the first at the back of the bag, thus forming a cone shape. Fold over the edges several times to secure the bag in place. Cut a small piece off the tip of the bag. Put in a little whipped cream and fold the top over.

INFORMAL MENUS

JAMBALAYA   *Serves 6*

This hot and gutsy dish from the southern states of America is a good choice for informal entertaining. Add as many chillies as you dare but one is probably enough for the average person! Serve with plenty of garlic bread.

Preparation time: 20 mins.   *Cooking time: 30 mins.*

2 tablsp oil
1 large onion, peeled and chopped
1 or more chillies (depending on taste), finely chopped
1 green pepper, sliced
2 sticks celery, sliced
2 cloves garlic, peeled and finely chopped
8 oz (225g) belly or pork strips, cut into small pieces
10 oz (285g) long grain rice
1 tablsp freshly chopped marjoram OR basil
14 oz (397g) can peeled tomatoes
6 oz (170g) smoked sausage, sliced
4 oz (110g) ham, sliced into strips
2 rounded teasp soft brown OR demerara sugar
Salt and freshly ground black pepper
1¼ pts (700ml) water
4 oz (110g) peeled prawns
3 spring onions, sliced

1. Heat the oil and fry the onion, chilli, green pepper, celery, garlic and pork for 10 minutes.

2. Add the rice and stir for a couple of minutes until translucent.

3. Stir in the herbs, tomatoes, sausage, ham, sugar, salt, pepper and water.

4. Bring to the boil, put a lid on the pan and simmer very gently for about 30 minutes until most of the liquid has been absorbed and the rice is tender.

5. Stir in the prawns and spring onions and cook for a further minute.

6. Turn into a large serving bowl.

Tip: Make up your own version of this recipe substituting various ingredients with whatever you can find at the right price. Strips of chicken for example could be used instead of pork or a couple of courgettes in place of the green pepper.

LEMON CRUNCH PIE   *Serves 6*

A tangy creamy filling in a crunchy biscuit case. A great favourite! The dish improves if made the day before eating.

Preparation time: 30 mins.   *Cooking time: None*

4 oz (110g) margarine
7 oz (200g) packet ginger nut biscuits
7 oz (200g) can condensed milk
Juice and finely grated rind of 2 large lemons
5 fl oz (150ml) carton double cream
1 small lemon for decoration

1. Melt the margarine in a medium sized saucepan.

2. Meanwhile, crush the biscuits by putting them in a small polythene bag and bashing with a rolling pin.

3. Tip the crushed biscuits into the margarine and mix very well.

4. Using the back of a wooden spoon press the mixture into a shallow 8″ (20.5cm) pie dish, making a case for the filling.

5. Put the condensed milk in a bowl and gradually whisk in the lemon juice and grated rind.

6. Whip the cream until it just holds its shape, but not too stiff, then fold it into the lemon mixture. (If liked a little can be reserved for piping some stars on the top.)

7. Pour the mixture into the biscuit case and chill for several hours before serving.

8. Decorate with thin slices of lemon.

LASAGNE

Serves 6

This is a popular choice for informal entertaining. Serve with garlic bread and a mixed salad of lettuce, watercress, cucumber, spring onions and tomato. Use lasagne marked, 'no pre-cooking required'.

Preparation time: 15 mins.   *Cooking time: 40 mins.*

1½ tablsp oil
1 large onion, peeled and chopped
6 oz (175g) button mushrooms, sliced
1 lb (450g) minced beef
1 tablsp flour
1 tablsp tomato purée
Salt and freshly ground black pepper
1 tablsp freshly chopped basil
14 oz (397g) can peeled tomatoes
¼ pt (150ml) water
Approx. 6 or 7 sheets lasagne
½ pt (300ml) cheese sauce (see page 31)
1 oz (25g) Cheddar cheese, grated (for topping)

1. Heat the oil and sauté the onion and mushrooms for 10 minutes.

2. Add the beef, breaking it down with a fork, and fry until brown, about 5 minutes.

3. Stir in the flour, tomato purée, salt, pepper, basil, tomatoes and water.

4. Mix well while bringing to the boil, then simmer for a couple of minutes.

5. Alternate layers of lasagne and meat mixture in a shallow ovenproof dish, ending with lasagne.

6. Pre-heat oven to 180°C (350°F) or Gas No. 4.

7. Make the cheese sauce as per page 31 and pour over the lasagne.

8. Sprinkle the grated cheese on top.

9. Bake for about 20 minutes until the cheese is brown and bubbly.

LEMON SORBET   *Serves 6*

Sorbets can be made so much more cheaply than buying and the lemon variety is one of the easiest. Serve with Continental-style wafers or delicate biscuits.

Preparation time: 10 mins.
    plus 12 hours freezing time   *Cooking time: 10 mins.*

8 oz (225g) caster sugar
1 pt (570ml) water
Thinly pared rind and juice of 3 lemons
2 egg whites

1. Dissolve the sugar in the water over a low heat.

2. Add the lemon rind and boil gently for 10 minutes.

3. Stir in the lemon juice and leave to cool.

4. Strain the liquid into a freezing tray or shallow dish and freeze until mushy.

5. Whisk the egg whites until stiff and then mix thoroughly into the lemon mixture.

6. Pour into a plastic lidded container and freeze for at least 12 hours before serving.

Tip: Use up the egg yolks in a quiche, bacon and egg pie, or omelette, or mix with a little milk and use to glaze pastry before cooking.

13. GIFTS GOOD ENOUGH TO EAT

If you are short of money, buying presents can be a nightmare. Everything is so expensive in the shops and five pounds goes nowhere. Yet home-made preserve, chutney and sweets look frightfully exclusive but cost just pence.

Edible gifts are suitable for young and old, male and female, a good friend or a chance acquaintance whether for Christmas, birthday, Mother's Day or as a special 'thank you' to a neighbour for feeding the cat.

Presentation is part of the secret. Go to town on pretty boxes and packets, shimmering metallic cartons, elaborate gift tags and a profusion of lacy paper doilies, ribbons and trimmings.

An added bonus is that you can top up your own stocks at the same time. Jams and chutneys should be made in summer and autumn when the ingredients reach rock bottom price. As long as all jars are adequately covered, chutney and jam should keep for up to 12 months. The recipes included here are pretty foolproof and don't require any elaborate or expensive equipment.

Savoury treats are just as welcome as sweet gifts. The

Smoked Mackerel Pâté on page 78 would be ideal. Remember however to add an 'eat me by' date label on perishables. Such gifts look particularly professional when presented in a china dish. Jumble sales and discount shops are good places to pick up cheap and attractive oddments.

TOMATO AND APPLE CHUTNEY

Make this delicious chutney in the autumn when tomatoes and cooking apples are at their cheapest. Chutney can be added to curries or served with sausages or cold meat. It's just right for the school bring and buy sale too!

Preparation time: 15 mins.   *Cooking time: 1½-2 hours*

4 lb (1.8kg) tomatoes
1 lb (450g) onions, peeled and chopped
1 lb (450g) cooking apples, peeled, cored and chopped
½ level teasp cayenne pepper
1 level teasp mixed spice
8 oz (225g) soft brown sugar
1 oz (25g) salt
¾ pt (425ml) malt vinegar

1. Peel the tomatoes by spearing with a fork and dipping them into boiling water for 1 minute: skins then peel off easily and can be discarded.

2. Cut the tomatoes into rough pieces and put them in a saucepan with all the other ingredients.

3. Bring to the boil then simmer gently for 1½-2 hours until thick and pulpy, stirring occasionally.

4. Pour into clean warm jars, cover with jam pot covers and label.

Tip: Throughout the year keep the jars, which are often attractively shaped, from ready-prepared tartare and horseradish sauce and the like. Cover with squares or rounds of material — stripes, checks or bold plain colours look best on savoury contents — and tie down with matching ribbon.

JAMS

Seasonal fruit is cheap and plentiful. It pays to ask your greengrocer if he has any jam quality fruit that he wants to get rid of. I did when I was writing this section and came away with an 11 lb box of cherries for the same price usually paid for 2 lb. What a bargain! Don't however buy any fruit which is too old, bruised or in bad condition.

Home-made jam is equal to the very best and most expensive preserves that are found in delicatessens and the results are easy to achieve.

Fruits with a low acid content are low in pectin which gives a soft set. Until fairly recently lemon juice, together with the pips tied in a muslin bag, were added to the fruit to give a firmer set. You can of course still use this traditional method, but special quick-set sugar with pectin is now available from larger supermarkets. It is excellent for fruit such as cherries, blackberries, apricots and strawberries. Not only does it give foolproof results but the jam is quicker to make because less boiling time is needed.

Ordinary granulated sugar is the most economical for acidic fruit such as raspberries, gooseberries, blackcurrants, redcurrants and plums. However, less scum is produced during boiling by using preserving or lump sugar.

Sometimes mould grows on jams, in which case it should be scraped off and discarded and the remainder eaten as soon as possible.

To test for set: Put a little jam on a cold saucer and allow to cool. Then push your finger across the surface, if the jam wrinkles and has slightly gelled, it is ready. If not, more boiling is needed.

You'll need:

Clean jam jars: Ask friends and neighbours to throw their empties in your direction rather than in the bin. Unusual shapes and sizes are particularly attractive if the jam is to be given as a present. The jars should be warmed before filling.

Packets of jam pot covers are available from stationers and kitchen-type shops. These include waxed discs, cellophane covers and rubber bands.

Labels: Pretty labels on which you can write the type of jam and the date it was made help convey a professional and attractive finish.

Decorative covers: Small fancy paper doilies tied down with ribbon, or use circles of pretty fabric.

CHERRY JAM
Makes about 6 lb (2.7kg)

Preparation time: 25 mins.   *Cooking time: 40 mins.*

4 lb (1.8kg) cherries
1 tablsp water
3½ lb (1.6kg) sugar with pectin

1. Stone the cherries and remove the stalks.

2. Put the cherries, water and any juice into a large saucepan.

3. Cook very gently over a low heat, prodding the cherries occasionally to release the juice, for about 30 minutes.

4. Add the sugar and stir until dissolved, then bring to the boil and boil rapidly for about 7-10 minutes until setting point is reached (see page 150). Leave to stand for 15 minutes.

5. Have ready some warmed jars.

6. Remove the scum from the jam, then pour into the jars, pop on a waxed disc and cover.

STRAWBERRY JAM
Makes about 5 lb (2.26kg)

Preparation time: 10 mins.   *Cooking time: 35 mins.*

Strawberry Jam continued

3 lb (1.4kg) strawberries
3 lb (1.4kg) sugar with pectin

1. Hull the strawberries, put them in a colander and rinse under cold water.

2. Tip the strawberries into a large saucepan and cook very gently until really soft, about 25 minutes.

3. Add the sugar and stir over a low heat until dissolved.

4. Bring to the boil and then boil rapidly for about 7-10 minutes until setting point is reached. (See page 150.) Leave to stand for 15 minutes.

5. Have ready some warmed jars.

6. Remove the scum and then stir the jam to distribute the strawberries evenly.

7. Pour into warmed jars, pop on a waxed disc and cover.

HELENSBURGH TOFFEE

This is not toffee in the true sense, more a textured fudge which the Scots call 'tablet'.

Preparation time: 20 mins.   *Cooking time: 1¼ hours*

2 oz (50g) butter
14½ oz (410g) can evaporated milk
Approx. ½ pt (300ml) milk
2 lb (900g) caster sugar
1 tablsp vanilla essence

1. Melt the butter in a large saucepan.

2. Pour the evaporated milk into a measuring jug and make up to 1 pint (570ml) with milk.

3. Add the milk and sugar to the pan and heat very gently until the sugar has dissolved. (The sugar must dissolve before the mixture boils.)

4. Boil fairly briskly until the mixture is brown in colour and reaches what is called 'soft ball'. This takes about 1¼ hours. Test by dropping a little mixture into a bowl of cold water: it should form a firm ball between thumb and forefinger.

5. Remove from the heat and stir in the vanilla essence.

6. Beat the mixture gently until it is thick and grainy, about 10-15 minutes.

7. Pour into an oiled tin, about 8″-10″ (20.5-25.5cm) square.

8. When almost set, mark into squares and then allow to go completely hard.

   Pack the tablet in clear cellophane or polythene bags and tie with ribbon if giving as a gift.

Tip: As a variation, add a couple of tablespoons of chopped walnuts to the mixture instead of vanilla essence.

MARZIPAN FRUITS

Stuffed dates and walnuts and marzipan fruits look professional when popped into small paper cases and packed into a shallow pretty box.

Preparation time: 1 hour   *Cooking time: None*

8 oz (225g) marzipan
Dates, stoned
Walnut halves
Caster sugar
Various food colourings

1. Make small balls of marzipan and press a walnut half on each side.

2. Make small pieces of marzipan into sausage shapes and substitute for the date stones. Roll the dates in caster sugar.

3. Divide the remainder of the marzipan into 4 and colour each orange, red, green or yellow. Use the colourings sparingly and knead well into the marzipan to ensure an even colour.

Surprisingly perhaps, it is not difficult to achieve professional-looking marzipan fruits; you don't have to be an artistic genius!

Apples: Roll pieces of green- and red-coloured marzipan into a ball so that the colours merge in a random manner.

Bananas: Roll pieces of yellow-coloured marzipan into banana shapes.

Lemons: Roll small pieces of yellow-coloured marzipan into a lemon shape. Then to simulate the skin, press all over the surface with a pin head or use a nutmeg grater or the fine side of a standard grater.

Oranges: Roll small pieces of orange-coloured marzipan into balls. Simulate the skin as with lemons.

Pears: Roll pieces of yellow- and green-coloured marzipan into a pear shape so that the colours merge in a random manner.

Stalks and Leaves: Roll out some green marzipan with a rolling pin. Cut out tiny leaves and then mark 'veins' with a sharp knife. Stalks can be made by rolling pieces of marzipan into tiny sausage shapes. Press stalks and one or two leaves on oranges, pears and apples.

TRADITIONAL SHORTBREAD

Shortbread is always popular at school-fund-raising days and if you plan to make it a lot, it is worth investing a few pounds in a traditional mould. These are available from specialist kitchen shops and produce an attractive and professional result.

Preparation time: 20 mins.   *Cooking time: 25 mins.*

3 oz (75g) butter (straight from fridge)
2 oz (50g) icing sugar, sieved
4 oz (110g) plain flour, sieved
Icing sugar to finish

1. Pre-heat oven to 170°C (325°F) or Gas No. 3.

2. Put the butter and icing sugar on a work surface and knead together until all the sugar has been absorbed.

3. Gradually knead in the flour until a smooth softish dough is formed.

4. Press the dough into a greased 7″ (18cm) sandwich tin or special shortbread mould, and bake for about 25 minutes until golden brown. Turn out when cool and dust with icing sugar.

INDEX

OUR PUBLISHING POLICY

HOW WE CHOOSE

Our policy is to consider every deserving manuscript and we can give special editorial help where an author is an authority on his subject but an inexperienced writer. We are rigorously selective in the choice of books we publish. We set the highest standards of editorial quality and accuracy. This means that a *Paperfront* is easy to understand and delightful to read. Where illustrations are necessary to convey points of detail, these are drawn up by a subject specialist artist from our panel.

HOW WE KEEP PRICES LOW

We aim for the big seller. This enables us to order enormous print runs and achieve the lowest price for you. Unfortunately, this means that you will not find in the *Paperfront* list any titles on obscure subjects of minority interest only. These could not be printed in large enough quantities to be sold for the low price at which we offer this series.

We sell almost all our *Paperfronts* at the same unit price. This saves a lot of fiddling about in our clerical departments and helps us to give you world-beating value. Under this system, the longer titles are offered at a price which we believe to be unmatched by any publisher in the world.

OUR DISTRIBUTION SYSTEM

Because of the competitive price, and the rapid turnover, *Paperfronts* are possibly the most profitable line a bookseller can handle. They are stocked by the best bookshops all over the world. It may be that your bookseller has run out of stock of a particular title. If so, he can order more from us at any time—we have a fine reputation for "same day" despatch, and we supply any order, however small (even a single copy), to any bookseller who has an account with us. We prefer you to buy from your bookseller, as this reminds him of the strong underlying public demand for *Paperfronts*. Members of the public who live in remote places, or who are housebound, or whose local bookseller is unco-operative, can order direct from us by post.

FREE

If you would like an up-to-date list of all *Paperfront* titles currently available, send a stamped self-addressed envelope to
ELLIOT RIGHT WAY BOOKS, BRIGHTON RD.,
LOWER KINGSWOOD, TADWORTH, SURREY, KT20 6TD, UK.